Do you prefer sunsh... or moonlight?

What's your favourite colour?

Curious
Questions & answers about...
The Solar System

Do you like warm weather better, or snow?

You're joining a space mission — what's your specialist skill?

If you could eat one food every day what would it be?

What's your FAVOURITE planet?

Words by Ian Graham

Illustrations by Barbara Bakos

MILES KELLY

Where is the Solar System?

It's all around you. The Solar System is the Sun, eight planets and everything else that moves through space with the Sun.

The planet we live on is called Earth. It's the third planet from the Sun.

Earth

Sun
In the middle of the Solar System is a star called the Sun.

Venus

Mercury

Moons
A moon is a small world that circles a bigger object – usually a planet. Earth has one, and it is made of rock.

Planets
Planets are the giant things like the Earth that travel round the Sun. There are eight in our Solar System.

The four planets closest to the Sun are small worlds made mostly of rock.

Mars

Zooooom!

Saturn

The four planets farthest from the Sun are giant balls of gas and liquid.

Uranus

Asteroid Belt

Jupiter

Neptune

Dwarf planets
Similar to planets in many ways, dwarf planets go round the Sun, but are not as big as planets.

Asteroids
Asteroids are rocky worlds smaller than planets. There are millions of them.

How do you make a solar system?

Our Solar System began as a huge cloud of gas and dust in space.

①

Dust and gas

How did the Solar System begin, and where did it come from?

First, an exploding star pushed against the cloud. The whole dusty cloud began to shrink.

③

So, there was a swirling disc of dust and gas – then what happened?

The dust and gas began to stick together, forming lumps that smashed into each other.

Lumps

Is the Sun hotter than an oven?

The Sun's surface is over 20 times hotter than a regular oven! The centre is even hotter – thousands of times hotter than an oven. It would melt the oven!

Surface

Core

NEVER NEVER look at the Sun. It's so bright and hot that it will hurt your eyes.

HYDROGEN

HELIUM

What is the Sun made of?

It's mostly made of stuff called hydrogen and helium. On Earth, hydrogen and helium are gases.

Why is the Sun bigger than other stars?

It isn't – the Sun is actually a small star. It looks much bigger than the other stars you see at night, because it is much closer to Earth than those other stars. They're all suns, but they are very far away.

Side-by-side with another star, I'm actually pretty tiny!

Scientists have found some suns that are 100 times bigger than the one in the Solar System!

Will the Sun be there forever?

No, but don't worry – it isn't going to disappear any time soon. The Sun should be there for another 5000 million years.

Where does the Sun go at night?

The Sun doesn't go anywhere – it's the Earth that is moving!

Our planet spins around an invisible line called the axis. It's daytime for you when the side you live on faces the Sun.

This spinning motion makes it look to us on Earth as if the Sun rises in the morning, crosses the sky, and then disappears at sunset.

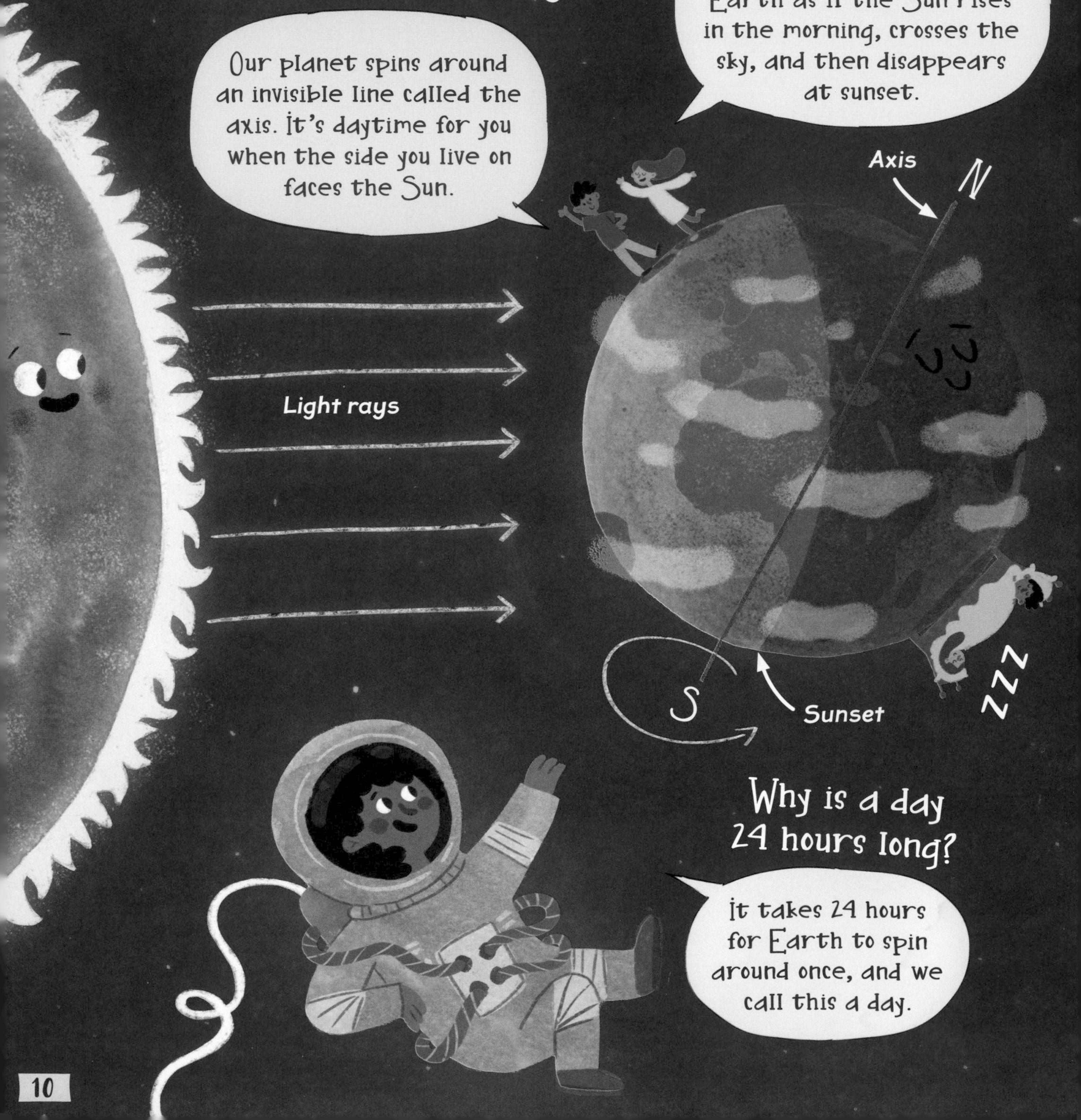

Axis

N

Light rays

S

Sunset

Why is a day 24 hours long?

It takes 24 hours for Earth to spin around once, and we call this a day.

ZZZ

Why do we have seasons?

Because Earth's axis is tilted. This means different bits of Earth get the Sun's direct rays at different times during Earth's orbit (journey around the Sun).

What is the Equator?

It's an invisible line that circles Earth. It divides it into a northern (top) half and southern (bottom) half.

Equator

In June, it's summer in the north and winter in the south.

In March, it's spring in the north, and autumn in the south.

N
S

N
S

N
S

N
S

In December, it's winter in the north and summer in the south.

In September, it's autumn in the north and spring in the south.

What is a year?

A year is the time it takes for the Earth to complete one orbit of the Sun.

Did you know?

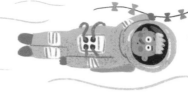

Jupiter has a huge storm called the Great Red Spot – it's about three times bigger than **Earth**.

Neptune is the Solar System's windiest planet, with winds ten times faster than the worst hurricanes on **Earth**.

Saturn is famous for its rings, but **Jupiter**, **Uranus** and **Neptune** have them too.

My rings are easy to see, because they're made of pieces of ice. Sunlight bounces off the ice and lights them up.

Our rings are thin, dark and dusty so they're hard to see.

The centre of the **Earth** is made of metal so hot that some of it has melted and turned to liquid.

You can jump six times higher on the **Moon** than you can on **Earth**.

Jupiter's moon **Ganymede** is the biggest moon in the Solar System – even bigger than the planet **Mercury**.

Dust storms are common on **Mars**. The sky there is pinky red, as so much red dust is blown about by the wind.

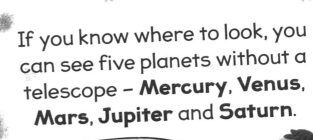

If you know where to look, you can see five planets without a telescope – **Mercury**, **Venus**, **Mars**, **Jupiter** and **Saturn**.

They are so far away they look like stars.

I'm only about half the width of the USA!

Astronauts who visited the **Moon** brought 382 kilograms of Moon rocks back with them.

Pluto was the Solar System's ninth planet – until 2006 when scientists decided to call it a dwarf planet instead.

There are between two and five solar eclipses every year.

Giant **Jupiter** spins so fast it has the shortest day of any planet – just 9 hours 55 minutes.

A solar eclipse happens when the **Moon** passes in front of the **Sun**. The Moon's shadow then moves across **Earth**, causing darkness to fall.

Are other planets like Earth?

Earth and the other three planets closest to the Sun are alike in some ways, but no other planet is exactly like Earth.

Why is it always so hot here?

Mercury is very hot because it's the closest planet to the Sun. It's smaller than Earth and it looks like the Moon.

Mercury

Why am i known as Earth's twin planet?

Venus

Venus and Earth are similar in size and structure – but the two planets look very different. Venus is wrapped in thick clouds of acid. They trap heat, so Venus is even hotter than Mercury.

What are the outer planets like?

The four planets farthest from the Sun – Jupiter, Saturn, Uranus and Neptune – couldn't be more different from Earth. They are giant worlds made of gas and liquid.

Jupiter

Saturn

Where did my rings come from?

How big am I?

Jupiter is the biggest planet in the Solar System. It's so big that more than a thousand Earths would fit inside it!

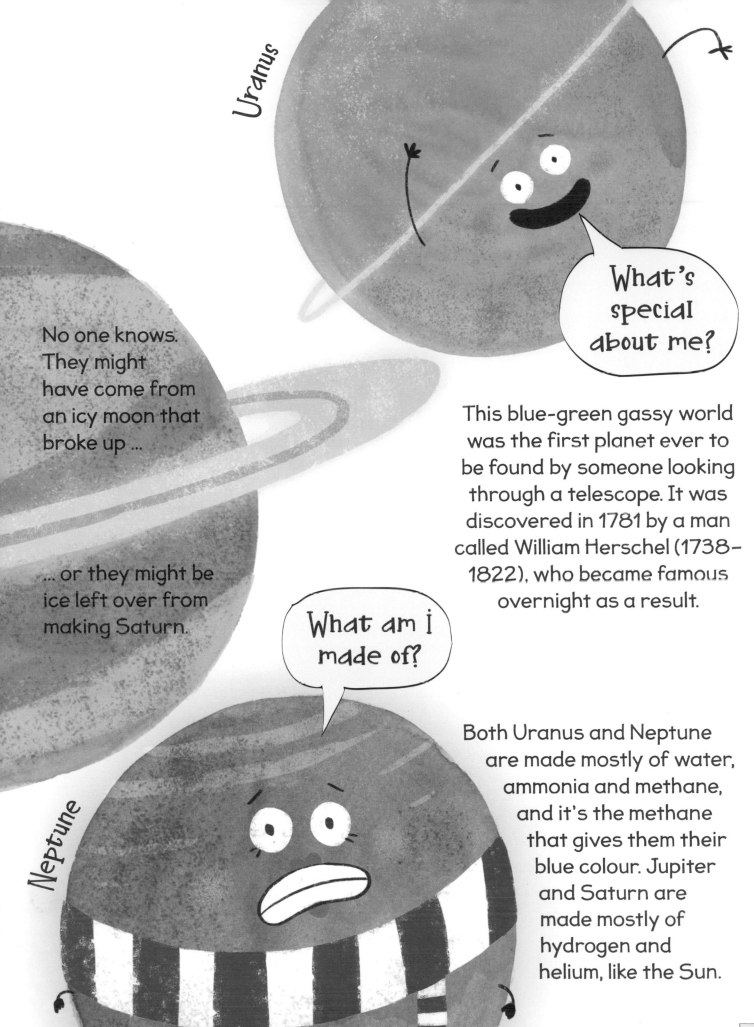

Uranus

No one knows. They might have come from an icy moon that broke up ...

... or they might be ice left over from making Saturn.

What's special about me?

This blue-green gassy world was the first planet ever to be found by someone looking through a telescope. It was discovered in 1781 by a man called William Herschel (1738–1822), who became famous overnight as a result.

What am I made of?

Neptune

Both Uranus and Neptune are made mostly of water, ammonia and methane, and it's the methane that gives them their blue colour. Jupiter and Saturn are made mostly of hydrogen and helium, like the Sun.

Do planets ever crash into each other?

Almost never. Billions of years ago, a planet the size of Mars crashed into Earth and sent lots of rock flying out into space. Can you guess what happened next?

1 A planet called Theia crashed into Earth.

2 The crash threw lots of rocks into space around Earth.

3 The rocks in space came together and became the Moon.

The Moon is the only place beyond Earth that humans have set foot on.

What's it like on the Moon?

The Moon is very dry and covered with grey dust. There are mountains, but there is no air, and the sky is always inky black.

Why is the Moon covered with craters?

These dents are made when rocks flying through space hit the Moon.

④ The Moon travels through space at a distance of 384,400 kilometres from Earth. Every year the Moon moves 4 centimetres further away from Earth.

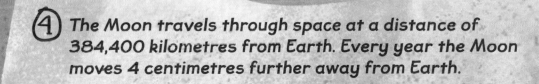

Would you rather?

Would you rather discover a new planet, like **William Herschel** did...

...or work out that all the planets in the Solar System orbit the Sun, like **Nicolaus Copernicus** did?

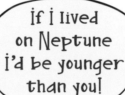

Would you rather live on **Earth** for your whole life, or spend your whole life in a **space station** where you could float about weightless?

If I lived on Mercury I'd be sixteen!

If I lived on Neptune I'd be younger than you!

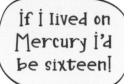

Would you rather kick a ball really far on the **Moon** or make a red sandcastle on **Mars**?

Would you prefer to live on **Mercury**, where a year lasts just 88 Earth days, or on **Neptune**, where a year lasts 165 Earth years?

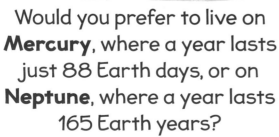

Which part of astronaut training would you rather do:

Work in a huge tank of water to practise **space walks**...

...or take a spin to get a feel for **extreme forces**?

If you had to name a new planet, would you rather call it **Aether**, after the Greek god of light, or **Erebus**, the god of darkness?

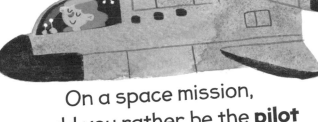

On a space mission, would you rather be the **pilot** flying the spacecraft, or a **specialist**, doing experiments and going on space walks?

Would you rather live on Uranus in **winter**, when the Sun doesn't rise for 20 years, or in **summer**, when it doesn't set for 20 years?

Would you rather slow down **Earth's** spin so days are longer, or move Earth closer to the **Sun** so that the weather is warmer?

What are shooting stars?

They're not stars! They're small pieces of rock that fly through space and into the air around Earth. Rubbing against the air heats them until they glow. They are also called meteors.

When lots of meteors appear in the sky, it's called a meteor shower.

Where do shooting stars go?

The smallest burn up and disappear. Others sometimes fall all the way down to the ground. If they land on Earth, they're called meteorites.

What happens when a big meteorite hits Earth?

It makes a hole in the ground called a crater. A famous crater in Arizona, USA, was made by a meteorite 50 metres across that hit the ground 50,000 years ago.

Why do comets have long, bright tails?

Comets are like giant dusty snowballs in space. If they fly near the Sun, some of the ice turns to gas and bursts out, carrying dust with it. The dust forms a tail that is lit up by sunlight.

How big are space rocks?

The biggest rocks in space are asteroids. Some can be up to 1000 kilometres across. Most asteroids are found in the Asteroid Belt between Mars and Jupiter.

How many?

-200° Celsius:

Brrrrrrrrr!

The average temperature on the Solar System's coldest planet, Neptune.

178 moons have been found going around planets so far. More might be found in future.

Life appeared on Earth about **4,000,000,000** years ago.

7,500,000,000: The number of people living on Earth.

0

The number of moons that the planets Mercury and Venus have.

The Solar System is about **4,600,000,000** years old.

The Solar System's tallest mountain is Olympus Mons on Mars. It's nearly **3** times the height of the tallest mountain on Earth, Mount Everest.

How many astronauts have walked on the Moon?

12

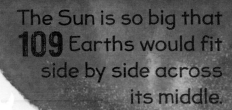

The Sun is so big that **109** Earths would fit side by side across its middle.

150 million kilometres: the distance from Earth to the Sun.

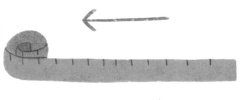

Halley's Comet appears in the sky every

76

years.

Just over **8** minutes: the amount of time it takes for sunlight to reach Earth.

165

The number of Earth years it takes the farthest planet, Neptune, to go once around the Sun.

3

...the number of days it takes astronauts to fly to the Moon in a spacecraft.

There are **5** dwarf planets in the Solar System. They are called...

Eris   Pluto   Haumea   Makemake   Ceres

How do we know about other planets?

No human has ever visited another planet, but we learn about them by sending robot spacecraft to study them. We have sent more spacecraft to Mars than any other planet.

Solar panels provide power

Robotic arm

I used my robotic arm to scoop up Martian soil to find out what it's made of.

Phoenix lander

Do spacecraft land on other planets?

Yes! Spacecraft that land on a planet are called landers. They take photographs of the surface and measure things like the temperature and wind speed. A spacecraft called Phoenix landed on Mars in 2008.

Mars Reconnaissance Orbiter

Powerful camera

How do we get good photos of Mars?

Robot spacecraft like me are called orbiters. We fly round and round it, like tiny moons. As we circle, we take photos and send them back to Earth by radio.

What is a rover?

Some of the spacecraft on Mars have wheels so that they can move around and explore more of the planet. They're called rovers. A rover called Curiosity landed on Mars in 2012.

Special instruments measure temperatures, wind speeds, radiation, and much more

My mission is to investigate Martian climate and geology, to find out whether Mars can support any life.

Curiosity

Is there life anywhere else?

Not that we know of – the search goes on. The spacecraft we have sent to other planets have been searching for signs of life there.

Erm... hello? Is anyone at home?

Why is there life on Earth?

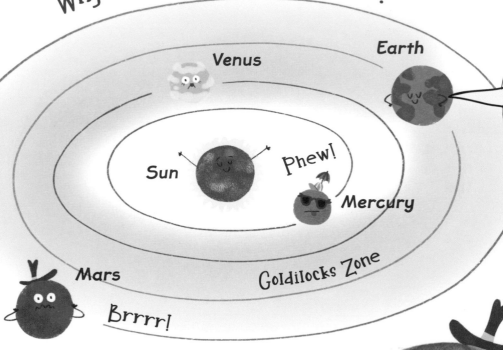

Venus

Earth

Sun

Phew!

Mercury

Mars

Brrrr!

Goldilocks Zone

My distance from the Sun means I have light, water and the correct temperature for life. I'm in what's called the 'Goldilocks Zone' – it's just right.

Why did people think aliens lived on Mars?

When people first used telescopes to study Mars they thought they saw lines on its surface. The idea spread that these were canals, made by aliens.

When spacecraft visited Mars, they found a dry, dusty planet with no canals – or aliens.

28

Is there water anywhere else in the Solar System?

Scientists think there may be oceans beneath the surfaces of some of Jupiter and Saturn's icy moons. Future missions will search for life there.

Europa

I'm one of Jupiter's moons. Scientists think I may have an iron core, a rocky middle layer and an ocean of salty water beneath my icy crust.

Rock

Metal

Water

Ice

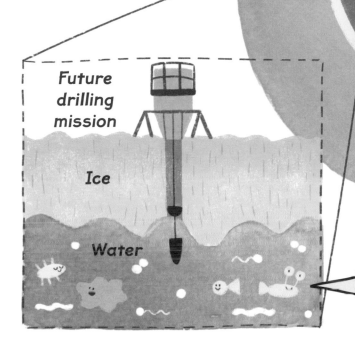

Future drilling mission

Ice

Water

Future missions will try to find out if Europa has an ocean, and may even drill through the ice. Who knows what they might find!

Where did Earth's water come from?

Some of it was already in the rocks that formed the Earth. The rest arrived as ice on comets and other space rocks that crashed into Earth soon after it formed.

A compendium of questions

Why aren't planets square?

Planets are round because of gravity. This special force pulls everything inwards, forming a ball shape.

Why is Earth called Earth?

It comes from an ancient word meaning land. Earth is the only planet that wasn't named after an ancient Greek or Roman god.

Where is the best view of the Sun?

Standing on Mercury when it is at its closest to the Sun, the Sun would appear more than three times as large as it does from Earth.

Which moon is the weirdest?

Hmmm... maybe Saturn's moon Enceladus. It spews jets of gas and ice from its south pole!

Are there rainbows on the Moon?

Sunlight and rain are both needed for a rainbow. There is no rain on the Moon, so you will never see a rainbow there.

Why is the Earth's sky blue?

As sunlight travels through air, the blue part of the light is scattered in all directions, so the sky looks blue.

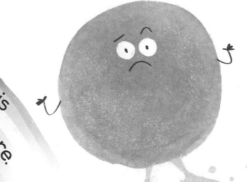

SUPER SKILLS

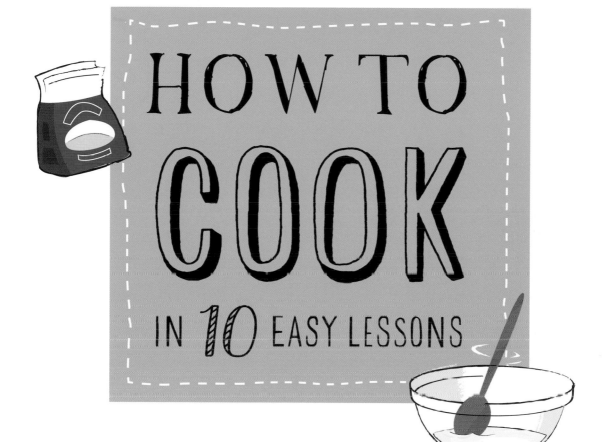

HOW TO COOK
IN 10 EASY LESSONS

WENDY SWEETSER

ABOUT THE AUTHOR

Wendy Sweetser has been a food writer for over 20 years, having trained at the Cordon Bleu cookery schools in both Paris and London. She began her career working for magazines, becoming Food Editor of Woman's Realm, TV Quick, and OK! Magazine. As well as developing recipes and food styling for editorial publications, Wendy works with several large food companies developing and publicising new products, and has written more than 25 cookery books.

PHOTO ACKNOWLEDGEMENTS

The publisher thanks the following photographers and agencies for their kind permission to use their images.

All photographs by **Ian Garlick**, with the exception of the following:

Stock food
Pages 35, 39, 45, 56, 61.

Shutterstock
Pages 5, 29 (baibaz); 8 (Piotr Kreslak); 10 (Julia Metkalova); 11 (Africa Studio); 14 (MaraZe); 15 (In Tune); 20 (Maxim Pushkarev); 21 (Olga Nayashkova); 22 (MaraZ); 26 (bonchan); 28 (RoJo Images); 33 (sumire8); 34 (Martin Turzak); 38 (bonchan); 46 (Elena Veselova); 51 (minadezhda); 54 (SGM); 55 (bernashafo).

First published in the UK in 2015 by
QED Publishing
Part of The Quarto Group
The Old Brewery
6 Blundell Street
London N7 9BH

www.qed-publishing.co.uk

A catalogue record for this book is available from the British Library.

ISBN: 978-1-78493-294-7 (spiral-bound edition)
ISBN: 978-1-78493-293-0 (flexi-bound edition)

10 9 8 7 6 5 4 3 2 1   15 16 17 18 19

Printed in China

Publisher: Zeta Jones
Associate Publisher: Maxime Boucknooghe
Art Director: Susi Martin
Managing Editor: Laura Knowles
Designer: Clare Barber
Original illustrations: Joanna Kerr
Principal Food Photographer: Ian Garlick

CONTENTS

INTRODUCTION   4

SUPER SKILL 1: USING KNIVES   6
- Rich Tomato Sauce for Pasta   8
- Minestrone Soup   9
- Vegetable Platter   10
- Super Fruit Salad   11

SUPER SKILL 2: PEELING & GRATING   12
- Pork Kebabs with Mint and
  Cucumber Raita   14
- Cheese Straws   15
- Key Lime Pie   16
- Apple Tarts   17

SUPER SKILL 3: CRUSHING & JUICING   18
- Homemade Fish Fingers   20
- Meatballs in Tomato Sauce   21
- New York Cheesecake   22
- Fresh Lemonade   23

SUPER SKILL 4: MASHING & PURÉEING   24
- Guacamole   26
- Hummus   27
- Cheesy Stuffed Potatoes   28
- Strawberry and Banana Smoothie   29

SUPER SKILL 5: FRYING,
SAUTÉING & BROWNING   30
- Stir-fried Chicken with Cashews   32
- Beef Tacos   33
- French Toast   34
- Hash Browns   35

SUPER SKILL 6: BOILING,
STEAMING & POACHING   36
- Eggs Benedict   38
- Perfect Pasta with a Creamy
  Mushroom Sauce   39
- Steamed Asian Dumplings   40
- Vegetable Fried Rice   41

SUPER SKILL 7: GRILLING,
ROASTING & BAKING   42
- Mini Pitta Pizzas   44
- Chicken Satay   45
- Chocolate Chip Cookies   46
- Roasted Mediterranean Vegetables   47

SUPER SKILL 8: MAKING SWEET
& SAVOURY SAUCES   48
- Apricot Coulis with Yoghurt
  and Toasted Oats   50
- Macaroni Cheese with
  Cherry Tomatoes   51

SUPER SKILL 9: BEATING,
WHIPPING & WHISKING   52
- Chocolate Sponge Cake   54
- Strawberry Pavlova   55
- Cheese Omelette   56
- Banana Bread   57

SUPER SKILL 10: MIXING, FOLDING
& KNEADING   58
- Seeded Bread Rolls   60
- Chocolate Mousse   61
- Carrot and Pecan Muffins   62

GLOSSARY OF EQUIPMENT   63

INDEX   64

INTRODUCTION

WELCOME TO THE KITCHEN!

So you want to be a super chef? It's not as difficult as you might think! All it takes is a pinch of practice, a dash of dedication and a good splash of energy. It's one of the most useful skills you'll ever master, and you'll have a lot of fun along the way.

ARE YOU READY?

Learning a new skill can be a bit daunting, so in this book we've chopped up the subject into the ten super skills you need to become a great cook. Each skill is accompanied by tasty recipes where you can try out the new techniques.

The more you cook, the more you'll enjoy it and want to experiment as you master a range of recipes. And – who knows? – what started out as a hobby could turn into your dream job when you grow up, with you as the next celebrity chef!

BE SAFE IN THE KITCHEN

- Always wash your hands before you begin preparing food.

- Have separate chopping boards for preparing meat, fish, and fruit and vegetables. Different coloured plastic boards such as red (meat), blue (fish) and green (fruit and vegetables) make it easy to pick the right one.

- When using the hob, keep your hands well away from gas flames or hot electric rings and take extra care with saucepans of hot liquid.

- Arrange the oven shelves in the position you need them before switching the oven on.

- Always wear thick oven gloves when removing a hot dish from the oven.

- Don't overfill dishes or pans with sauce that could spill or boil over. Not only will spills make the oven or hob dirty, they could splash your hands and burn them.

- Cook's knives need to be sharp for chopping and slicing ingredients, so take extra care when using them. Keep your fingers out of the way!

STAY SAFE!
MAKE SURE THERE IS AN ADULT NEARBY TO HELP YOU STAY SAFE, ESPECIALLY WHEN USING SHARP KNIVES, A KETTLE OR THE OVEN.

MAKING LIFE EASIER FOR YOURSELF

- Always read a recipe all the way through before you begin.

- Get out the ingredients and weigh the quantities you need.

- Decide what equipment you need to make your recipe and get these out before you begin.

- Do initial preparation like chopping onions, carrots, peeling potatoes and trimming fat from meat before you start cooking.

- Keep your work surface tidy as you go along by clearing up peelings and returning butter or milk to the fridge once you've finished with them.

- Put empty cans, jars, utensils and plates you've used by the sink, ready to be washed up when you've finished cooking.

- Taste your recipe as you cook – all the best chefs do! It's the only way you can check if a dish needs more sugar, a pinch of salt or an extra squeeze of lemon juice.

CHECK YOUR SKILLS

You'll see boxes like this one on every recipe page. If you're unsure of some of the cooking skills you need to use, you can easily find the page where the technique is explained.

You will need

Here is a list of basic equipment you'll need to try out the recipes in this book:

Grater

Whisk (balloon or electric)

Liquidizer or blender

Food processor

Wooden and large metal spoons

Measuring jug & spoons

Ice cream scoop

Cake and bread pans
    (made of metal or silicone)

Sieve and colander

Knives for chopping and slicing

Chopping boards

Can opener

Baking sheets or trays

Roasting tin

Mixing bowls in different sizes

Saucepans with lids

Frying pans

Casserole dish with a lid

Kitchen scissors

Potato masher

Scales

Vegetable peeler

Rolling pin

Baking parchment

Pastry brush

Foil, kitchen roll and cling film

DON'T FORGET YOUR APRON, OVEN GLOVES AND TEA TOWELS!

SKILL 1

USING KNIVES

Learning how to use a kitchen knife correctly is not difficult, but it is an important skill for any chef to learn, and essential to avoid cutting yourself.

Always ask an adult's permission to use a knife. Make sure you are sitting comfortably at a table and that the chopping board is steady. Hold the food firmly in place, with your fingers well away from the blade. Cut slowly and steadily and, if the task is a little difficult, ask an adult to help you. Always be very careful with knives, and lay them flat and out of the way when you are not using them.

CHOOSING THE RIGHT KNIFE

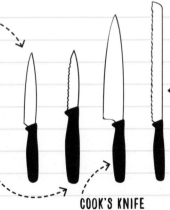

KITCHEN KNIFE
Used for peeling, slicing and dicing. Not suitable for cutting large items due to its short blade.

SMALL SERRATED KNIFE
Perfect for cutting crusty rolls, tomatoes and fruit where you need the knife to 'bite' into the items.

COOK'S KNIFE
You can cut almost anything with this knife, and it comes in a range of sizes, from medium to large.

BREAD KNIFE
The serrated or scalloped edges can cut through a hard crust but won't damage the loaf's soft interior as the bread is sliced.

CHOPPING BOARDS
These can be made of wood, thick plastic, or bendable plastic. It is best to cut meat on a plastic chopping board as wood is slightly absorbent but all types should be washed thoroughly with hot, soapy water after use.

Technique 1: CUTTING A TOMATO INTO WEDGES

Tomatoes are used in lots of different recipes where their vivid red colour and sweet flavour makes them a popular ingredient.

1 Using a small serrated knife, carefully saw through the tomato vertically.

2 Place one half of the tomato on a board, cut side down. Cut through the rounded top, angling the knife towards the centre. Repeat 2–3 times.

3 Repeat Step 2 for the remaining tomato half. If you don't want to eat the seeds scoop them out with a small spoon.

Technique 2: SLICING AN ONION

Onions can be small or large, round or oval and pale gold, red or pure white in colour but they are all prepared in the same way.

Hold everything really firmly

KEEP YOUR FINGERS AWAY FROM THE KNIFE BLADE.

1 Rest the onion on its side and grip it to keep it steady. Cut off the top of the onion.

2 Using the tip of the knife, peel off the onion skin and trim off the root end.

3 Hold the onion so that it is sitting on the root end. Keeping the onion steady cut it in half, straight to the root. Turn it round and repeat on the other side to make two halves.

4 Lie one of the halves flat on the board and slice through the onion four times or more in a forward-cutting motion, until you reach the centre. Turn it round and repeat holding carefully as the knife reaches the centre.

5 To cut an onion into small pieces, hold a slice of onion firmly with your fingers and cut across the slice so that it forms little 'cubes' of onion.

Slice up the other half of the onion in the same way.

Technique 3: CUTTING CARROTS INTO CUBES

Like tomatoes, carrots are great for adding colour and flavour to all sorts of recipes from soups and stews to stir-fries and salads.

try to cut pieces a similar size

1 Peel the carrot using a vegetable peeler (see page 13) and then cut off the leafy green top and the tip of the root end.

2 Lay the carrot down on a chopping board and, holding it at the top, cut through the middle, starting at the centre and going down to the tip. Turn the carrot around and cut through the other way from the centre to the top to make two halves. Then cut each in half again lengthways.

3 Cut across each quarter of the carrot to make small cubes, holding the thickest end of the carrot and keeping your fingers well away from the blade of the knife.

4 For carrot sticks to dip into hummus, cut the carrot halves lengthways, then into 1-cm-wide strips.

RICH TOMATO SAUCE *for pasta*

This is one of the tastiest and easiest pasta sauces to make. Serve it spooned over your favourite pasta shape, topped with grated Parmesan cheese.

INGREDIENTS

- 1 onion, peeled
- 2 cloves of garlic, peeled
- 2 tbsp olive oil
- 2 x 400 g (14 oz) cans of chopped tomatoes
- 1 tbsp tomato purée
- 1 tsp sugar
- Black pepper
- 1 handful of fresh basil leaves, chopped
- Parmesan cheese, to serve

1 Slice the onion and chop up the slices. Crush the garlic with a rolling pin or wooden spoon.

2 Heat the oil in a pan on the hob on a low heat. Cook the onion for 10 minutes, adding the garlic for the last 2 minutes.

CHECK YOUR SKILLS

- p. 7 for slicing an onion
- p. 13 for grating cheese
- p. 31 for sautéing
- p. 36 for cooking on the hob

3 Stir in the tomatoes, tomato purée and sugar. Grind in some black pepper and stir well. Lower the heat, cover the pan with a lid and leave to simmer gently for 15 minutes. Stir in the basil.

4 Cook your pasta according to the packet instructions. Drain, divide between 4 plates and spoon the sauce on top. Serve with a generous sprinkling of grated Parmesan cheese.

Yummy

SERVES 4

TRY THIS!

You can use different types of pasta such as spaghetti, fusilli or penne. Add different ingredients, such as 50 g chopped black olives, 4 chopped anchovy fillets, 50 g chopped bacon fried with the onion or a pinch of dried chilli flakes. You could also use fresh tomatoes, instead of tinned.

MINESTRONE *Soup*

Hearty soups, like this very popular one from Italy, are often described as 'knife and fork soups' since they are thick, chunky and a meal in themselves.

INGREDIENTS

- 1 tbsp olive oil
- 1 onion, peeled and sliced
- 2 carrots, peeled and chopped
- 3 sticks of celery, chopped
- 2 garlic cloves, peeled and chopped
- 400 g (14 oz) can chopped tomatoes
- 2 tbsp tomato purée
- 1.2 l (2 pt) chicken or vegetable stock, made with stock cubes
- 400 g (14 oz) can cannellini beans, drained and rinsed under cold water
- 100 g (3½ oz) spaghetti, broken into short lengths

YOU WILL NEED

Cook's knife

Chopping board

Colander

Large saucepan with a lid

Large spoon

1 Heat the oil in a large saucepan and cook the onion and carrots over a low heat for about 10 minutes, stirring occasionally with a large spoon, until the vegetables have softened.

2 Add the celery and garlic, fry for 1 minute and then stir in the chopped tomatoes, tomato purée and stock.

CHECK YOUR SKILLS

- p. 7 for slicing onions
- p. 7 for chopping carrots
- p. 31 for frying and sautéing
- p. 36 for boiling

3 Bring to the boil, reduce the heat to a simmer. Put a lid on the saucepan and simmer the soup for 15 minutes.

4 Add the cannellini beans and spaghetti and simmer for a further 10 minutes or until the pasta is tender.

5 Ladle the minestrone into soup bowls and serve with chunks of crusty bread.

TRY THIS!
The Italians like topping this soup with grated Parmesan, sprinkling the cheese over the soup after it has been spooned into bowls.

SERVES 6

VEGETABLE PLATTER

Raw vegetables cut into batons and arranged on a large platter are known as crudités and they make a very colourful and tasty snack to serve at parties. Serve with a bowl of dip, such as guacamole or hummus (see recipes on pages 26 and 27).

YOU WILL NEED

Cook's knife

Chopping board

Colander

Kitchen paper

Serving platter

INGREDIENTS

- ½ cucumber
- 1 red pepper
- 1 green pepper
- 1 carrot
- 3 sticks of celery

TAKE CARE WHEN USING A SHARP KNIFE.

CHECK YOUR SKILLS

- p. 6–7 for choosing the right knife and slicing vegetables

TRY THIS!

As well as cucumber, peppers, carrots and celery, you can also add whole radishes, button mushrooms and tiny cauliflower florets to your vegetable platter.

1 Cut the cucumber into quarters lengthways. You can remove the seeds or leave them in as you prefer. Cut each quarter into 6–7 cm lengths and then slice each piece into thin batons.

2 Slice the peppers into quarters lengthways. Cut away the stalks and the membranes inside with the seeds attached to them. Put the peppers in a colander and run cold water over them to wash away any remaining seeds. Pat the peppers dry on kitchen paper and cut each quarter lengthways into batons the same size as the cucumber.

3 Cut any leaves off the top of the celery and pull away the loose 'strings' running down the sticks, as these will be unpleasant to eat. Cut the sticks into 6–7 cm lengths and then slice into batons the same size as the cucumber and peppers.

4 Cut the carrot by following steps 1 and 2 on page 7. Then cut the quarters lengthways into batons of a similar size to your other vegetables.

5 Arrange the vegetables on a serving platter, making individual piles of the different vegetables, and serve with a dip. If not serving immediately, cover the vegetables with cling film to prevent them drying out.

SERVES 6–8

SUPER FRUIT SALAD

Mmm... tasty and healthy! You can use the fruits suggested here or, if you prefer, choose a selection of your favourite ones. The more colourful the combination of different fruits, the better your fruit salad will look.

INGREDIENTS

- 150 ml (¼ pt) apple juice
- 1 canteloupe melon
- 2 kiwi fruit
- 2 pineapple slices
- 225 g (8 oz) strawberries
- 100 g (3½ oz) blueberries

YOU WILL NEED

Measuring jug Chopping board
Cook's knife Kitchen knife
Large spoon
Glass serving bowl

CHECK YOUR SKILLS

- - - - - - - - - - - - - - - -
- p. 6 for choosing the right knives to chop, peel and slice

1 Cut the melon in half with a cook's knife, scoop out the seeds with a spoon and discard them. Cut each half into four wedges and peel by sliding the knife round each wedge between the flesh and the rind.

2 Cut each wedge into bite-sized pieces, being careful to keep the wedge steady on your chopping board, and your fingers away from the knife.

QUICK TIP... It's quite hard work to peel and chop up a whole pineapple. Unless you want to make a really big fruit salad to feed lots of people, it's easier to buy ready-prepared slices, or you could try tinned pineapple.

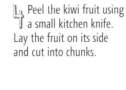

3 Chop the pineapple slices into bite-size pieces.

4 Peel the kiwi fruit using a small kitchen knife. Lay the fruit on its side and cut into chunks.

5 Pull the hulls off the strawberries and cut large fruit into halves or quarters.

so delicious

6 Put all the prepared fruit, plus the blueberries, into a glass bowl and pour the apple juice over the fruit. Cover the bowl with cling film and chill until ready to serve.

SERVES 6-8

PEELING AND GRATING

Peelers and graters are both important tools in a cook's kitchen, as they can be used to perform lots of different tasks. A peeler removes the skin quickly and easily from cucumbers, apples and pears, or root vegetables such as potatoes, swedes and parsnips. A grater can be used to shred hard cheese and vegetables such as carrots and courgettes, or to remove the zest from citrus fruits.

TYPES OF PEELER AND GRATER

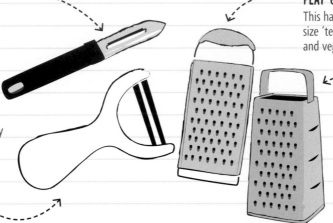

FIXED-BLADE VEGETABLE PEELER

Hold the non-slip handle and draw the cutting blade of the peeler over a fruit or vegetable to remove the skin in thin, even strips.

SWIVEL-BLADE PEELER

Can be used in the same way as a fixed-blade peeler, but shaving off long, thin slices of a vegetable is easier. The swivel blade makes it suitable for both left- and right-handed cooks.

FLAT GRATER

This has a single grating surface with medium size 'teeth' for grating hard cheese, chocolate and vegetables.

BOX GRATER

As its name suggests, this grater is shaped like a tall box with a handle on top to hold it steady. It has a different grade of grating surface on each side – for example, medium for cheese and fine for citrus fruit zest.

Technique 1: PEELING A CUCUMBER

When peeling any kind of vegetable or fruit, it's important to just remove the thin, outer layer of skin so that none of the flesh is cut away and wasted.

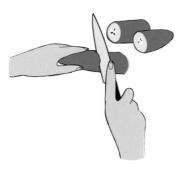

1 Cut the cucumber in half or quarters or leave whole, depending on how much you need for your recipe.

2 Holding the cucumber at one end, draw the cutting blade of the peeler over the skin to shave off a long, thin strip.

3 Continue around the cucumber, peeling off the skin in strips until it has all been removed.

Technique 2: GRATING CHEESE WITH A BOX GRATER

You can only grate hard and semi-hard cheeses such as Cheddar and Parmesan. Soft, creamy cheeses will crumble and block up the teeth of the grater.

1 Hold the grater upright with one hand over a plate or bowl.

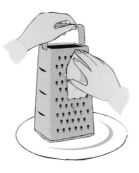

2 With the other hand, rub a block of cheese down the grating surface – making sure your fingers are kept well away from the teeth as they are very sharp.

3 Hold the grater as steady as you can so that, as the cheese is grated, the flakes are collected on the plate or inside the grater.

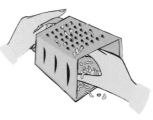

4 Reach inside the grater to remove any cheese stuck there. Shake the grater to remove any pieces of cheese from the outside.

Technique 3: GRATING FRUIT ZEST WITH A BOX GRATER

When lemon, lime or orange rind needs to be added to a recipe, use the finest surface of a grater. Only grate the colourful outer zest and leave behind the white pith, which has a bitter taste. If you can, use unwaxed fruit.

1 Wash the fruit in warm water and dry with a sheet of kitchen paper.

2 Stand the grater upright on a plate and steady it by holding the handle on top.

3 Keeping the fruit whole, rub the skin over the finest surface of the grater to remove the zest, grating until the white pith is just visible and turning the fruit as you go.

4 When all the zest has been removed, use a brush to remove any still clinging to the teeth of the grater. Don't try to remove it using your fingers, as you could cut yourself on the sharp teeth.

PORK KEBABS with Mint and Cucumber Raita

YOU WILL NEED

- Cook's knife
- Chopping board
- Spoon
- Fork
- Grater
- 8-12 metal or wooden skewers
- Pastry brush
- Mixing bowl

Kebabs are fun to eat and marinating the ingredients before you thread them onto the skewers gives the kebabs extra flavour. They go perfectly with raita, a cool yoghurt dip. Raita is a popular dish in India, where it is served with spicy curries.

INGREDIENTS

FOR THE KEBABS:
- 500 g (1lb 2 oz) lean pork loin steaks
- 2 tbsp olive oil
- 2 tbsp orange juice
- 1 tbsp clear honey
- 1 red pepper
- 2 courgettes

FOR THE RAITA:
- 200 g (7 oz) thick natural yoghurt
- 8 fresh mint leaves, finely chopped
- ¼ cucumber, peeled and grated

CHECK YOUR SKILLS
- p. 6 for using knives
- p. 12 for peeling
- p. 42 for grilling

TRY THIS!
When the weather is warm outside, you can grill the kebabs on a barbecue. Experiment by trying out different types of meat and vegetables on your kebabs.

1 Trim any fat from the pork steaks and cut the meat into 2.5 cm cubes.

3 Cut the pepper in half and deseed it, then cut it into 2.5 cm pieces. Trim off the tops and bottoms of the courgettes and cut into bite-size pieces.

4 Add the pork and vegetables to the bowl and stir until coated with the orange and honey mixture. Leave in a cool place to marinate for 1 hour, stirring occasionally.

SERVES 4

6 Preheat the grill to high and grill the kebabs for 6–7 minutes, turning them over once or twice, or until the pork is cooked and the vegetables are browned at the edges. If any marinade is left in the bowl, brush this over the kebabs as they cook.

QUICK TIP... If you use wooden skewers, soak them in a bowl of cold water for 30 minutes beforehand or cover the exposed ends with small pieces of foil to prevent them burning on the grill.

2 Put the olive oil, orange juice and honey into a mixing bowl and whisk the ingredients together with a fork until evenly combined.

5 Thread the pork, pepper and courgette pieces alternately onto the skewers. Lay the kebabs side by side in a single layer in a grill pan – line the pan first with foil to make light work of the washing up afterwards!

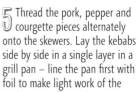

7 Make the raita by putting the yoghurt in a small bowl and stirring in the grated cucumber and chopped mint. Serve with the kebabs.

CHEESE STRAWS

These tasty, savoury biscuits are delicious on their own as a snack or served with soup. This recipe uses a mixture of mature Cheddar and Parmesan, but feel free to use other hard cheeses with a strong flavour, if you prefer.

YOU WILL NEED

Grater
Mixing bowl
Cook's knife
Sieve
Baking sheet
Parchment
Rolling pin
Cling film
Fish slice

INGREDIENTS

- 150 g (5 oz) mature Cheddar cheese
- 50 g (2 oz) Parmesan cheese
- 375 g (13 oz) plain flour, plus a little extra for dusting
- 225 g (8 oz) butter, diced
- 1 large egg, beaten

CHECK YOUR SKILLS

- p. 13 for grating cheese

1 Grate the Cheddar and Parmesan cheeses onto a plate.

2 Sieve the flour into a mixing bowl and, using your fingertips, rub in the butter until there are no lumps of butter left and the mixture looks like fine breadcrumbs. Stir in the grated cheeses, the beaten egg and 4 tablespoons of cold water.

QUICK TIP... The butter will be much easier to rub into the flour if you take it out of the fridge about 30 minutes before you want to make the cheese straw dough. This will allow the butter to come to room temperature and soften a little.

3 Use your hands to bring the ingredients together to form a ball of dough, adding a little more cold water if needed. Wrap the dough in cling film and chill in the fridge for 30 minutes to firm it up.

4 Preheat the oven to 190°C/ 375°F/gas 5. Dust the work surface with a little flour, transfer the dough to it and roll it out to a square about 5 mm thick.

TRY THIS! For a spicy kick, sieve 1 teaspoon of chilli powder or paprika into the mixing bowl with the flour.

5 Cut each square in half and then cut each half into 1 cm strips. Take one strip of pastry and twist it two or three times. Carefully lift it onto the baking sheet and press the ends of the strips down lightly. Repeat with all the remaining strips of dough and then bake them for 10–15 minutes until crisp.

6 Leave the cheese straws to cool on the baking sheet before lifting them off with a fish slice.

MAKES ABOUT 36

KEY LIME PIE

This rich and creamy pie from Florida is traditionally made using the key limes that are native to the sunshine state. If you can't find key limes, ordinary limes will still make a scrumptious pie.

YOU WILL NEED

Large measuring jug

Mixing bowl

Plastic bag and rolling pin or food processor

Balloon whisk

Large metal spoon

Saucepan

23 cm pie dish

Baking sheet

INGREDIENTS

FOR THE PIE CRUST:
- 225 g (8 oz) digestive biscuits
- 125 g (4 oz) unsalted butter

FOR THE PIE FILLING:
- 400 g (14 oz) can sweetened condensed milk
- 4 egg yolks
- 200 ml (7 fl oz) double cream
- finely grated zest of 2 limes
- 100 ml (3½ fl oz) freshly squeezed lime juice

CHECK YOUR SKILLS
- p. 13 for grating citrus zest
- p. 19 for juicing citrus fruit
- p. 19 for crushing biscuits
- p. 42–43 for using the oven

1 To make the pie crust, preheat the oven to 200°C/400°F/gas 6. Crush the biscuits to crumbs either in a plastic bag using a rolling pin or in a food processor. Transfer the crumbs to a mixing bowl.

2 Melt the butter in a saucepan over a low heat and tip it into the biscuit crumbs. Mix well and then spoon the crumbs into the pie dish, pressing them down firmly with the back of the spoon so they cover the base and come up the sides of the plate.

3 Put the pie dish on a baking sheet, bake the crust for 10 minutes and then remove it from the oven. Lower the oven temperature to 170°C/325°F/gas 3.

4 To make the filling, put the condensed milk in a large jug, add the egg yolks and whisk together until combined. Stir in the double cream, lime zest and lime juice.

5 Carefully pour the filling into the cooked crust and bake the pie for 15 minutes.

6 Allow the pie to cool completely and then chill it in the fridge for 2–3 hours before serving.

TRY THIS!
Cut the pie into wedges to serve, topping each serving with a spoonful of whipped cream and a fresh lime wedge.

QUICK TIP... It is easiest to squeeze the juice out of limes if you soften them first. Grate the zest off the limes and then put them in the microwave and give them a 5-second burst on full power.

SERVES 8

APPLE TARTS

These tarts make a really impressive dessert, especially if you serve them with whipped cream or scoops of vanilla ice cream. Make up one large tart and cut it into individual portions before serving.

YOU WILL NEED

Baking sheet

Cook's knife

Pastry brush

Chopping board

Saucepan

INGREDIENTS

- 375 g (13 oz) sheet of ready-rolled puff pastry
- 1 egg, beaten
- 3 tbsp ground almonds
- 3 tbsp golden caster sugar
- 3 dessert apples
- 50 g (2 oz) unsalted butter
- 3 tbsp apricot jam
- 3 tbsp chopped almonds

1 Unwrap the pastry and lay it on a baking sheet. Brush the top of the pastry all over with the beaten egg to glaze.

2 Mix the ground almonds with 1 tablespoon of the sugar and scatter this over the pastry. With a knife, score the pastry into six equal pieces, without cutting all the way through the pastry.

CHECK YOUR SKILLS

- p. 6 for using knives
- p. 12 for peeling
- p. 42–43 for using the oven

3 Peel the apples, cut into quarters and remove the cores. Slice each quarter lengthways into thin slices.

4 Arrange the apple slices over the pastry, between the score lines. Scatter the remaining sugar over the apples.

5 Cut up the butter into small pieces and dot over the apples. Preheat the oven to 200°C/400°F/gas 6 and bake for 25–30 minutes or until the pastry is puffed and golden brown and the apples are soft.

6 Warm the apricot jam in a small saucepan over a low heat and brush the jam over the apples. Scatter the chopped almonds on top. Cut the tart into portions along the scored lines and serve warm.

Delicious...

QUICK TIP... When brushing the pastry with beaten egg, take care not to let the egg run down the sides of the pastry. If this happens, the layers in the pastry will stick together and won't rise up and become beautifully crisp and flaky in the oven.

TRY THIS!
You can also make the tarts using shortcrust pastry if you prefer. If using a block of pastry, roll it out on a board dusted with flour to a rectangle measuring about 20 x 30 cm (8 x 12 in) and trim the edges with a cook's knife to neaten them. Top with the almonds and apples and bake in an oven at 180°C/350°F/gas 4 for 45 minutes.

SERVES 6

CRUSHING AND JUICING

A food processor is useful for taking the hard work out of lots of kitchen jobs, such as making breadcrumbs or mincing meat. However, many tasks, such as crushing digestive biscuits to make crumbs for the base of a cheesecake, are easy to do by hand and you don't need any special equipment.

THE FOOD PROCESSOR

Food processors do lots of tasks, from chopping and slicing to mixing, puréeing, blending and grating.

The ingredients to be processed are put straight in the machine's bowl, with the cutting or mixing attachment fitted. Once the lid of the bowl has been clipped firmly in place, the motor is switched on and the food is mixed or chopped. Alternatively, the ingredients can be pushed or fed down the upright tube attached to the lid with the motor running. This method is used when you are slicing or grating cheese or vegetables such as carrots and courgettes. It can also be used for adding a liquid gradually to a pastry or bread dough or a dressing such as mayonnaise.

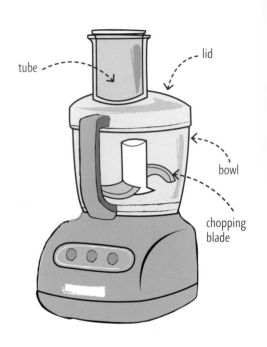

tube

lid

bowl

chopping blade

TYPES OF JUICER

this is a handy piece of equipment to have in your kitchen.

JUICE EXTRACTOR
You can use this type of machine to extract juice from lots of different fruit and vegetables, such as mangos or carrots.

SIMPLE CITRUS JUICE PRESS
This is a shallow-sided dish that has a ridged dome on top in the centre. It is very easy to use to squeeze the juice from citrus fruits such as lemons, small oranges and limes.

HAND-CRANKED CITRUS JUICE PRESS
These are larger machines designed to extract the juice from big oranges, grapefruits and pomelos.

Technique 1: MAKING BREADCRUMBS

Making breadcrumbs is a great way to use the end of a loaf when it's a little past its best. It's easy, too: all the bread can be processed in one go.*

ASK AN ADULT HELP YOU WHEN HANDLING A FOOD PROCESSOR BLADE.

1 Weigh out the quantity of bread you need. It's best to use bread that is a few days old, once it has become a little dry.

2 Tear or cut the bread into pieces, removing the crusts first or leaving them on, if you prefer.

3 Place the bowl in position on the food processor, fit with the double-sided chopping blade and put the bread in the bowl before clipping the lid on top.

4 Switch the motor on and process the bread to fine crumbs.

5 Transfer the crumbs to a bowl, scraping out any that are trapped in the corners of the food processor's bowl.

❉ You can make biscuit crumbs in a food processor too, but they must be fed one-by-one down the tube.

Technique 2: CRUSHING BISCUITS BY HAND

Do this on a hard surface such as a chopping board. Seal the bag so that the crumbs don't shoot out of the top, and hold the bag steady – making sure you keep your hand well away from the rolling pin, of course!

1 Put the biscuits in a large or medium-sized freezer bag and push out most of the air before you seal it, in case the bag bursts when you hit it with the rolling pin.

2 Put the bag of biscuits on a chopping board. Hold the bag with your hand so it doesn't move around on the board as you make the crumbs.

3 Bash the biscuits in the bag firmly with a rolling pin to break them into small pieces. Continue to hit the biscuits until they are reduced to crumbs. Open the bag and tip the crumbs into a bowl.

Technique 3: JUICING A CITRUS FRUIT

When using a juice press, the juice either collects in the dish around the dome or the dish will have draining holes and sit above a bowl for the juice to flow into.

1 If using a simple citrus juice press, cut small citrus fruit, such as a lemon, lime or orange in half through the centre.

2 Put half the fruit, cut side down, over the dome and press down firmly, twisting the fruit as you press to extract the juice.

1 If using a hand-cranked citrus juice press, put halves of fruit cut-side down in the press.

2 Pull down the handle or turn it, depending on the style of machine you are using. The juice that runs out collects in the jug or bowl that comes with the machine.

HOMEMADE FISH FINGERS

YOU WILL NEED

Food processor
2 large plates and
1 shallow bowl
Cook's knife
Fish slice
Fork
Chopping board
Large frying pan
Kitchen paper

Fancy making fish fingers from scratch? It's super easy. You can use any firm white fish, but thicker fillets such as cod or haddock work better than flat fish such as plaice or sole.

INGREDIENTS

- 450 g (1 lb) thick white fish fillets
- 6 slices of stale white bread, crusts removed
- 4 tbsp plain flour
- 1 egg
- oil for shallow frying

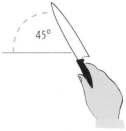

1 Place the fish fillets skin side down on a chopping board. Using a cook's knife, work the blade between the skin and the flesh of the fish at the tail end of a fillet to loosen the flesh from the skin. Holding the knife with the blade away

from you and a 45-degree angle, move the blade backwards and forwards down the fillet so the flesh comes away from the skin in a single piece. Repeat with the remaining fillets and cut the flesh into 8 strips, across the grain of the flesh.

CHECK YOUR SKILLS

- p. 6 for using knives
- p. 19 for using a food processor
- p. 30 for shallow frying

2 Tear up the bread slices into smaller pieces, put in the food processor bowl with the chopping blade fitted and the lid on top. Process for about 30 seconds, or until the bread becomes fine crumbs. Tip out the crumbs onto a large plate and spread out the flour on another plate.

TRY THIS!
Mix the breadcrumbs with 1 teaspoon of dried thyme or ½ teaspoon of a spice such as paprika or ground coriander before coating the fish.

3 Crack the egg into a shallow bowl and beat lightly with a fork.

4 Coat the fish fingers with flour and then with beaten egg before putting them on the plate of crumbs and patting the crumbs all over them. Chill the fish fingers until you are ready to cook them.

5 Heat about 4 tablespoons of oil in a large frying pan, add the crumbed fish fingers and fry over medium heat for 5–6 minutes or until golden, turning over occasionally so they cook evenly. Drain from the pan with a fish slice onto a plate lined with kitchen paper.

6 Serve the fish fingers while they're hot, with lemon wedges to squeeze over them and some tartare sauce or tomato ketchup.

SERVES 4

QUICK TIP... Use an oil with a neutral flavour to fry the fish sticks, such as sunflower, rapeseed or groundnut oil.

MEATBALLS in Tomato Sauce

You can prepare these tasty meatballs ahead and chill them in the fridge on a plate covered in cling film until you are ready to cook them. Serve them with mashed potatoes and vegetables or spoon them over pasta.

YOU WILL NEED

Large spoon

Cook's knife

Large bowl

Spatula

Frying pan

INGREDIENTS

FOR THE MEATBALLS:
- 4 tbsp olive oil
- 1 small onion, peeled and chopped as finely as you can
- 500 g (18 oz) lean minced beef
- 50 g (2 oz) breadcrumbs (see Fish Fingers recipe, page 20)
- 1 egg, beaten
- Ground black pepper
- A little plain flour, for dusting

FOR THE TOMATO SAUCE:
- 1 quantity of Rich Tomato Sauce for spaghetti (see page 8)

1 Heat 1 tablespoon of the olive oil in a frying pan over a gentle heat. Add the chopped onion, cover the pan and cook for about 5 minutes until the onion is soft and turning golden. Drain the onion from the pan and set aside to cool.

2 In a large bowl, mix together the minced beef, breadcrumbs and cold cooked onion, breaking up any lumps of meat with a spoon.

3 Stir in the beaten egg and season with lots of ground black pepper.

CHECK YOUR SKILLS

- p. 7 for chopping onions
- p. 8 for making tomato sauce
- p. 30–31 for frying and sautéing

QUICK TIP... The meatballs can be made with lean lamb or pork mince if you prefer.

4 Dust your hands with flour, divide the mixture into 12 and shape into round balls. Chill in the fridge until ready to cook.

5 Heat the remaining oil in the frying pan and fry the meatballs for about 5 minutes, shaking the pan occasionally so they brown all over.

TRY THIS!
When cooked, spoon the meatballs and tomato sauce into a shallow ovenproof dish, top with 150 g (5 oz) grated mozzarella cheese and place under a hot grill until the cheese melts and bubbles.

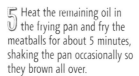

6 Spoon out any excess oil from the frying pan before pouring the tomato sauce over the meatballs. Bring the sauce to the boil, lower the heat under the pan and simmer for 15 minutes. Serve hot with mash and vegetables or spooned over pasta.

SERVES 4

NEW YORK CHEESECAKE

This classic cheesecake has a buttery biscuit base that melts in the mouth. Just the sort of dessert to make if you're trying to 'butter' up your parents!

YOU WILL NEED

20 cm spring clip cake tin

Baking sheet

Saucepan

Large spoon

Mixing bowl

INGREDIENTS

FOR THE BASE:
• 50 g (2 oz) unsalted butter
• 200 g (7 oz) digestive biscuits, crushed

FOR THE TOPPING:
• 250 g (9 oz) full fat cream cheese
• 250 g (9 oz) ricotta cheese
• 175 g (6 oz) caster sugar
• 4 large eggs
• 1 tsp vanilla extract
• 300 ml (½ pt) full fat soured cream

CHECK YOUR SKILLS

• p. 19 for crushing biscuits
• p. 52 for beating

SERVES 6-8

1 To make the base, melt the butter in a saucepan, remove the pan from the heat and stir in the biscuits crumbs.

2 Spoon the crumbs into a 20.5 cm spring clip cake tin and press over the base with the back of the spoon. Chill in the fridge while you make the topping.

3 To make the topping, in a large bowl, beat together the cream cheese and ricotta cheese with half the sugar until evenly mixed.

4 Beat in the eggs, one at a time, followed by the vanilla.

5 Pour this mixture over the biscuit base and stand the tin on a baking sheet.

6 Preheat the oven to 150°C/ 300°F/gas 2 and bake the cheesecake for an hour. Remove it from the oven and leave to stand for 5 minutes.

7 Stir the rest of the sugar into the soured cream and pour over the cheesecake. Return it to the oven for 5 minutes, then remove the cheesecake and leave it to cool completely before removing from the tin.

Scrumptious

TRY THIS!
For a special treat, serve the cheesecake with either chocolate sauce or fruit coulis drizzled over each serving. Go to pages 48 and 49 to find out how to make these delicious toppings.

QUICK TIP... Instead of vanilla, you could flavour the cheese with lemon. Stir the grated zest from 1 large or 2 small lemons into the cream cheese mixture and leave out the vanilla extract.

FRESH LEMONADE

This is very easy to make and it is the perfect summer drink for picnics on the beach or barbecues in the garden. Add some ice cubes or crushed iced to each glass before pouring in the lemonade.

INGREDIENTS

- 4 large, unwaxed lemons
- 100 g (3½ oz) caster sugar

TO SERVE:
- 1 litre sparkling mineral water or soda water
- Ice cubes or crushed ice

YOU WILL NEED

Vegetable peeler   Cook's knife
Large jug   Bowl   Two forks
Citrus juicer
Tall glasses, to serve

1 Using a vegetable peeler, cut away the zest from each lemon in strips, working from the top to the bottom of a lemon until it is all removed. Put the strips in a bowl.

2 Cut the zested lemons in half and squeeze the juice.

CHECK YOUR SKILLS
- p. 12 for peeling
- p. 19 for juicing

TRY THIS!
To give your lemonade a pretty pink colour, add a dash of grenadine to the jug.

3 Add the juice to the bowl along with the caster sugar, stirring until the sugar dissolves. Leave to stand for 30 minutes so the zest adds extra flavour to the juice.

4 With a fork, lift out the zest and discard.

So refreshing!

5 Pour the juice mixture into a large jug and top up with the sparkling mineral water or soda water. Stir to combine.

6 Half fill tall glasses with ice cubes or crushed ice and pour in the lemonade.

SERVES 4

QUICK TIP... Be careful to just peel away the thin layer of yellow zest from the lemons and leave the bitter white pith behind.

MASHING AND PURÉEING

Have you ever tried to mash potatoes with a fork? You can do it, but it's not much fun! It's far quicker and easier to use a proper masher, as you'll get a smoother and creamier result. It's also easy to whizz up a smoothie or a soup if you have a blender. Here's all the info you need to master Super Skill Number 4!

TYPES OF BLENDER AND MASHER

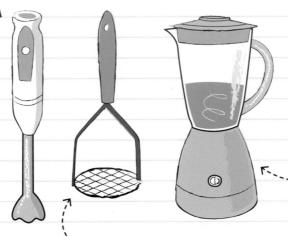

HANDHELD BLENDER
This handy machine is also known as a stick blender. It has a long, round shaft that is easy to hold in one hand, with a small, revolving blade attached to the other end. Some blenders come with a beaker that can be used for blending small amounts of ingredients.

GOBLET BLENDER
This free-standing blender is made up of a stand, which contains the motor, and a clear plastic goblet that sits on top. The goblet has a revolving blade in the bottom and a tight-fitting lid. When blending fruit or vegetables in a goblet blender, you need to add a liquid such as stock or fruit juice, or the blender won't purée them smoothly.

HAND MASHER
This is used to turn cooked vegetables such as potatoes, carrots, swedes, parsnips and peas to a smooth, lump-free mash.

Technique 1: USING A GOBLET BLENDER TO BLEND SOUP

Goblet blenders are mainly used for puréeing vegetables to make soups and fruit to make smoothies.

1 Simmer the ingredients, such as chopped vegetables or pulses, in stock or water until they are very tender. Leave to cool as you could burn yourself if you blend the mixture while it is still very hot.

2 Clip the goblet in place on its stand. Spoon enough of the soup mixture into the goblet to fill it about half full.

3 Fit the lid on top and keep your hand on the lid as you blend to ensure it stays firmly in place. Turn the switch on the stand to full speed and blend the mixture until it is smooth.

4 Pour the purée into a clean saucepan, ready to be reheated. Blend the rest of the soup in the same way.

Technique 2: USING A HANDHELD BLENDER TO PURÉE FRUIT

As well as puréeing fruit and vegetables, handheld blenders are useful for doing all sorts of kitchen jobs, such as making smoothies, whipping cream, whisking pancake batter and making sure a gravy or sauce isn't lumpy.

1 Prepare the fruit as necessary by peeling and removing cores, stones and stalks. Chop the flesh to be puréed into evenly sized pieces. If you are only blending a small quantity, place the fruit pieces in a blender beaker. If you are blending a larger quantity, put the fruit into a mixing bowl.

2 Plug in the blender if necessary and, holding it directly upright, put the blade in the fruit. Make sure the blade is completely covered by the fruit to avoid any splatters flying up while you are blending.

3 Press the on/off button on the shaft of the blender and keep the blade immersed in the fruit until it becomes a smooth purée. Switch off before lifting out the blade.

4 Use a spatula to scrape out the purée and wash the blender head under the tap.

Technique 3: MASHING POTATOES

Before they can be mashed, the potatoes must be steamed or boiled until they are very tender – but not disintegrating. Test if they are done by piercing them with a fork. You can also mash other root vegetables.

Make sure they're nice and soft

1 If boiling the vegetables, drain them thoroughly when cooked and return to the saucepan. If steaming, transfer them to a dry pan.

2 Hold the masher upright and push the grid-like head into the soft vegetables.

3 Lifting the masher up and then pushing it down quite firmly, work your way around the pan until all the vegetables are crushed and reduced to a smooth mash.

3 For a tasty, creamy mash, add a knob of butter and a splash of milk while you're mashing the vegetables.

GUACAMOLE

YOU WILL NEED

Chopping board

Spoon

Cooks knife

Two bowls

Hand masher or fork

Handheld blender

This can be spooned onto burgers and jacket potatoes, served with fajitas or tacos (see recipe on page 33) or used as a dip with tortilla chips. It is traditionally quite spicy but you can reduce the number of chillies – or add more if you like things hot!

INGREDIENTS

- 3 red chillies
- Small bunch of coriander leaves
- 2 medium tomatoes, finely chopped
- 1 small onion, peeled and finely chopped
- Juice of 2 limes
- 3 ripe avocados

TAKE EXTRA CARE WITH CHILLIES!

The heat from chillies comes from the seeds and membranes inside. They can give a nasty burning sensation if you touch your face or rub your eyes with your fingers after preparing them. To avoid this, use a fork and small sharp knife so your fingers don't come into contact with the chillies or wash your hands immediately afterwards.

1 Cut the stalks off the chillies and slit them open lengthways. Scrape out the seeds and membranes inside and chop the flesh finely.

CHECK YOUR SKILLS

- p. 6 for using knives
- p. 25 for puréeing and mashing

QUICK TIP... Once avocado flesh is exposed to the air it starts to turn brown. To keep the guacamole looking nice and green, drizzle a little lemon or lime juice over the top after spooning it into a serving bowl. Then press cling film over the surface.

2 Coarsely chop the coriander leaves.

Snack time!

3 Put the chillies, coriander, half the chopped tomatoes, onion and the juice of 1 lime in a bowl and blend until you have a fine paste.

4 Cut the avocados in half lengthways, remove the stones and scoop out the flesh into a mixing bowl using a spoon.

5 Mash the avocado flesh coarsely with the rest of the lime juice, using a hand masher or fork.

6 Stir in the chilli paste and the rest of the tomato until evenly mixed. Spoon into a small serving bowl and chill until ready to serve.

SERVES 6

HUMMUS

Hummus is made by blending together chickpeas, lemon juice, garlic and a paste made from ground sesame seeds called tahini. It is served as a dip with vegetable crudités (see recipe on page 10) or fingers of warm pitta bread. Hummus originates from the Middle East but it is now popular all over the world.

INGREDIENTS

- 400 g (14 oz) can chickpeas, drained and rinsed under cold water
- 3 tbsp lemon juice (or to taste)
- 3 garlic cloves, skinned and finely chopped or crushed
- 3 tbsp tahini (sesame seed paste)
- 3 tbsp water
- 1 tbsp extra virgin olive oil
- salt and pepper, to taste

TO SERVE:
- 2 tbsp extra virgin olive oil
- 1 tsp paprika

YOU WILL NEED

Colander for rinsing the chickpeas

Cook's knife or garlic press

Large spoon

Citrus press

Goblet blender or handheld blender

1 Put the chickpeas in a goblet blender or bowl and add the lemon juice, garlic, tahini, water and olive oil.

2 Blend everything together until the mixture is very smooth. Taste the hummus and adjust the flavour if necessary – you may need to add a little more lemon juice. Season with a little salt and pepper as well.

CHECK YOUR SKILLS

- p. 19 for juicing lemons
- p. 24–25 for using a goblet blender or handheld blender

QUICK TIP... You can also scatter some toasted pine kernels over the hummus before you serve it. To toast the kernels, spread them out on a baking sheet and place in a 170°C/325°F/gas 3 oven for 4–5 minutes until they are golden. Turn them over halfway through, so they toast evenly. When the nuts are ready, remove them from the baking sheet straight away or they might burn.

3 Spoon the hummus into a small bowl or spread it out on a flat plate, levelling the top with the back of the spoon.

4 To serve, drizzle the olive oil over the top of the hummus and dust with the paprika.

SERVES 6

CHEESY STUFFED POTATOES

YOU WILL NEED

Baking tray
Skewer

Cook's knife

Mixing bowl

Spoon

Hand masher

Fork

These baked potatoes are great for a fireworks party or Halloween, especially if it's a cold night and everyone is hungry!

INGREDIENTS

- 2 large baking potatoes
- 125 g (4 oz) grated Cheddar cheese
- 4 tbsp milk
- 125 g (4 oz) cooked ham, cut into small pieces
- Freshly ground black pepper

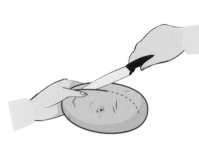

CHECK YOUR SKILLS

- p. 6 for using knives
- p. 12 for grating cheese
- p. 25 for hand mashing
- p. 43 for baking

QUICK TIP... When scooping out the potato flesh, leave about 3 mm (1/8 in) of the flesh attached to the skin to support it. Take care not to break the skins as you scoop.

1 Preheat the oven to 180°C/350°F/gas 4. Wash the potatoes and pat dry with kitchen paper. Using a sharp knife, score a line just through the skin lengthways around the centre of each potato.

2 Put the potatoes in a baking tray and bake for 1 hour or until they are tender. Test they are ready by pushing a skewer into the centre of each. Leave the potatoes to cool.

3 Cut the potatoes in half along the scored lines and scoop out the flesh into a bowl with a spoon. Mash the potato flesh with a hand masher.

4 Add the milk, cheese and ham to the mashed potato and stir until evenly mixed. Season with black pepper.

5 Spoon the mixture into the potato shells, pressing it down with a fork and mounding it up a little in the centre. Put the potato shells back on the baking sheet and return to a 180°C/350°F/gas 4 oven for 30 minutes or until piping hot.

TRY THIS!
Instead of ham, you could add other ingredients to the mashed potato – try cooked, chopped bacon, finely chopped spring onions or sweetcorn kernels.

SERVES 4

STRAWBERRY and BANANA SMOOTHIE

Everyone loves a cool, creamy smoothie! Once you've made one yourself, you'll never want to go back to drinking the shop-bought kind.

INGREDIENTS

- 1 banana
- 150 g (5 oz) strawberries
- 375 ml (13 fl oz) milk
- 125 g (4 oz) strawberry or natural yoghurt

YOU WILL NEED

- Chopping board
- Cook's knife
- Handheld stick blender
- Measuring jug
- Large bowl
- 3-4 tall glasses

1 Peel the banana and cut it into three or four pieces.

2 Wash the strawberries and pat them dry with kitchen paper. Remove the green hulls and chop large fruit into halves or quarters.

3 Put the banana and strawberries in a jug and add the milk and yoghurt.

4 Blend until smooth. Pour into tall glasses and serve.

CHECK YOUR SKILLS

- p. 6 for using knives
- p. 25 for puréeing using a handheld blender

SERVES 3-4

QUICK TIP... On a hot day, don't forget to add a couple of ice cubes to each glass before serving or chill the glasses in the fridge for 1 hour first.

FRYING, SAUTÉING AND BROWNING

Frying or sautéing on the hob are quick ways to cook all kinds of foods. Different types of pans are used to fry eggs or make an omelette, fry potatoes for hash browns, sear a steak or stir-fry chicken and vegetables for a Chinese feast.

CHOOSING THE RIGHT PAN FOR THE JOB

FRYING PANS

Frying pans are wide pans with a flat base and shallow sides. They come in different sizes and can be made of stainless steel, with or without a non-stick coating, or cast iron. They are used on the hob to fry ingredients such as meat, fish, eggs and vegetables in a small amount of oil. Frying can be done over a medium or high heat, depending on the recipe.

WOKS

Chinese woks are deep pans that have a long handle and rounded base. Like frying pans, they come in a variety of sizes and are made from different materials such as carbon steel, stainless steel and aluminium.

Woks are used for stir-frying ingredients in a tiny amount of oil over a high heat. Meat, seafood and vegetables are first cut into small, even-sized pieces and then tossed continuously in a wok with a metal spatula so they cook very quickly and evenly. Other ingredients, such as rice and noodles, are pre-cooked in another pan before being added.

WATCH OUT!

Extra care needs to be taken when cooking with hot oil. If food is dropped into the pan, the oil could splash up and burn your hand or catch fire if it comes into contact with a gas flame. Always ask an adult to help.

SAUTÉ PANS

These are similar to frying pans but have deeper sides and a lid so ingredients such as onions can be softened or 'sweated' over a low heat with the lid on, and then browned with the lid removed and the heat increased.

Technique 1: FRYING SAUSAGES

When frying sausages you can add a little oil to the pan or dry fry them without any oil if you prefer.

Be careful when heating oil in a pan.

1. If your sausages are linked together, snip them apart with kitchen scissors but avoid pricking the skins of the sausages with a fork as they could split when you fry them.

2. Place a frying pan on the hob over a medium heat and add 1 tablespoon of a flavourless oil such as groundnut, sunflower or vegetable oil.

3. When the pan is hot, carefully place the sausages in the pan, one at a time, making sure they are not touching each other.

4. Cook for 8–12 minutes, depending on how large the sausages are. Turn over occasionally with tongs or roll over by shaking the pan, so that the sausages brown evenly on all sides.

Technique 2: SAUTÉING ONIONS

Sliced or chopped onions are best cooked in a sauté pan over a low heat with the lid on the pan to begin with so that they soften and all their sweet flavour is released.

1 Peel your onions and chop or cut them into thin slices (see page 7).

2 Heat a sauté pan on the hob over a low heat and add 2 tablespoons of oil. This can be a flavourless oil or it can be olive oil, which will add its own flavour to the onions as they cook.

3 Add the chopped onions, put the lid on the pan and sauté the onions over a low heat for about 15–20 minutes until they are really soft but haven't turned brown.

4 Take the lid off the pan and stir the onions occasionally with a large spoon or spatula so they soften evenly.

5 Once the onions are soft, remove the lid and raise the heat to medium. Cook for a further 5–10 minutes until the onions are golden brown, stirring them frequently so they don't stick to the bottom of the pan and burn.

Technique 3: BROWNING BEEF

When making a casserole, you need to brown the pieces of meat first in hot oil so the outsides of them become caramelized and all their flavour and juices are sealed in. This can be done in a sauté pan (without the lid on) or in the casserole dish you are using, so long as it is flameproof – such as one made of stainless steel or cast iron – and is suitable to go on the hob as well as in the oven.

1 Trim any fat from your meat – this can be beef, pork or lamb – and, using a large cook's knife, cut the meat into 2.5 cm cubes. Wash your hands.

2 Put the pan on the hob over a fairly high heat and add 1 tablespoon of a flavourless oil.

WASH YOUR HANDS AFTER HANDLING RAW MEAT.

3 When the oil is hot, add five or six pieces of meat to the pan, using a large spoon and wearing an oven glove, as the cold meat could make the hot oil spit.

4 Stir the meat occasionally so the pieces brown on all sides. Lift them out with the spoon and transfer to a plate lined with kitchen paper. Repeat with the remaining pieces. If the pan becomes dry, add a little more oil to stop the meat from sticking.

STIR-FRIED CHICKEN with Cashews

If you like Chinese food, you'll love this tasty combination of tender chicken, crunchy nuts and crisp vegetables.

YOU WILL NEED

Cook's knife

Chopping board

Vegetable peeler

Wok

Spatula or slotted spoon

Large plate

Small bowl

Measuring jug

Whisk

Measuring spoons

Serving platter

INGREDIENTS

- 3 tbsp oil
- 75 g (3 oz) unsalted cashews
- 4 boneless, skinless chicken breasts, cut into 2 cm (3/4 in) cubes
- 1 red onion, peeled and sliced
- 1 carrot, peeled and cut into thin sticks
- 1 green pepper, deseeded and chopped
- 2 tsp sweet chilli sauce
- 2 tbsp light soy sauce
- 1 tsp cornflour
- 175 ml (6 fl oz) chicken stock

1 Heat 1 tablespoon of the oil in the wok and stir-fry the cashews for about 30 seconds until lightly browned. Remove the cashews with a metal spatula or slotted spoon, and set aside on a plate.

2 Add another tablespoon of the oil to the wok and stir-fry the chicken over a fairly high heat for 5 minutes or until golden. Remove to the plate.

CHECK YOUR SKILLS

- p. 6–7 for using knives
- p. 12 for using peelers
- p. 30 for stir-frying

3 Add the remaining tablespoon of oil and stir-fry the onion and carrot for 3 minutes. Add the green pepper and stir-fry for a further 3 minutes.

4 Return the cashews and chicken to the wok and add the chilli sauce.

5 In a small bowl, whisk the soy sauce with the cornflour until smooth and then add the stock.

QUICK TIP... Make sure the oil is nice and hot before you add your ingredients to the wok.

TRY THIS!
Instead of chicken, you could use cubed lean pork or large raw peeled prawns. If using prawns, only stir-fry them for 2–3 minutes until they turn pinkish-white, as they cook more quickly.

6 Pour into the wok and toss everything together over the heat for 2–3 minutes until the sauce is bubbling. Serve at once.

SERVES 4

BEEF TACOS

Tex-Mex food is tasty and fun to eat, so dishes like these beef tacos make the perfect finger food to tuck into at a party.

INGREDIENTS

FOR THE BEEF FILLING:
- 1 tbsp sunflower or groundnut oil
- 450 g (1 lb) lean beef mince
- 1 green pepper, deseeded and chopped
- 1 quantity of Rich Tomato Sauce (see recipe on page 8, leaving out the Parmesan cheese)

TO SERVE:
- 12 taco shells
- 1 quantity of Guacamole (see recipe on page 26)
- 3 tomatoes, diced
- 1 small lettuce, shredded
- Grated Cheddar cheese

YOU WILL NEED

Baking sheet
Large spoon
Spatula
Sauté pan
3 small serving bowls

1 To make the beef filling, heat the oil in a sauté pan, add the mince and fry until browned.

2 Add the green pepper, fry for 5 minutes and then add the tomato sauce. Simmer uncovered for 15 minutes, stirring occasionally.

CHECK YOUR SKILLS

- p. 7 for slicing an onion
- p. 6 for cutting a tomato
- p. 13 for grating cheese
- p. 31 for sautéing

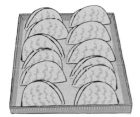

3 When ready to serve, preheat the oven to 180°C/350°F/gas 4. Spread out the taco shells on a baking sheet and warm through in the oven for 3–4 minutes.

4 Spoon the guacamole, shredded lettuce, diced tomatoes, and grated cheese into separate serving bowls.

QUICK TIP... Stir the beef mince occasionally as it browns, breaking up any lumps with your spatula.

SERVES 4

5 Spoon the mince into the taco shells and leave diners to spoon their own guacamole, lettuce, chopped tomatoes and grated cheese on top.

TRY THIS! Instead of beef mince, make the filling with turkey or lamb mince.

FRENCH TOAST

YOU WILL NEED

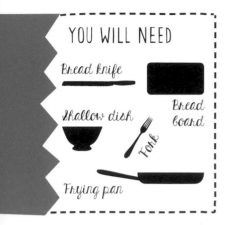

Bread knife

Shallow dish

Bread board

Fork

Frying pan

For a real treat, make French toast for breakfast. You can drizzle it with maple syrup and serve it with a rasher of crisp-fried bacon alongside, or sprinkle the cooked toast with a little brown sugar and serve it with fresh fruit. Yum!

INGREDIENTS

- 4 slices of white bread
- 1 egg
- ½ tsp ground cinnamon
- 50ml (2fl oz) milk
- 15 g (½ oz) unsalted butter

1 Cut the slices of bread in half diagonally to make 8 triangles in total.

2 In a shallow dish, beat together the egg, milk and cinnamon with a fork until evenly mixed.

CHECK YOUR SKILLS

- p. 6–7 for using knives
- p. 30 for frying

QUICK TIP... Make sure the triangles of bread are completely coated in the egg mixture so they are beautifully golden when fried.

3 Heat the butter in a frying pan over a medium heat.

4 As soon as the butter has melted, dip each triangle of bread in the egg mixture until coated on both sides.

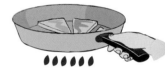

5 Add the eggy bread to the pan and fry for 1 minute on each side until golden brown. Serve at once.

6 You can also add some fruit to your French toast. Try using raspberries, blueberries, strawberries or banana slices.

TRY THIS!
Instead of cinnamon, add 1 teaspoon vanilla extract to the egg and milk.

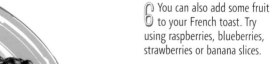

SERVES 4

HASH BROWNS

Hash Browns are great served for brunch with scrambled eggs, bacon, tomatoes and, of course, ketchup!

INGREDIENTS

- 4 medium potatoes, peeled
- 1 onion, peeled and finely chopped
- 1 egg, beaten
- Salt and pepper
- 3 tbsp groundnut, sunflower or vegetable oil

YOU WILL NEED

Clean tea towel
Large plate lined with kitchen paper
Grater
Fish slice
Palette knife
Mixing bowl
Frying pan
Tablespoon

1 Lay a clean tea towel on the work surface and grate the potatoes onto this.

2 Twist the towel around the potatoes and squeeze it over the sink to remove excess liquid.

CHECK YOUR SKILLS

- p. 7 for chopping onions
- p. 13 for using a grater
- p. 30 for frying

3 Put the potatoes in a mixing bowl and stir in the chopped onion and beaten egg, mixing well so the potatoes and onion are coated with the egg. Season with a little salt and some pepper.

4 Heat the oil in a large frying pan and add tablespoons of the potato mixture, flattening down each mound with the back of the spoon to make a patty about 1 cm thick.

QUICK TIP... When grating the potatoes, take care not to let your fingers get too near the teeth of the grater. When only about a quarter of a potato is left, push this onto a fork before continuing to grate.

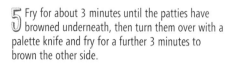

5 Fry for about 3 minutes until the patties have browned underneath, then turn them over with a palette knife and fry for a further 3 minutes to brown the other side.

TRY THIS!

Add some finely chopped red pepper and sliced salad onions or a finely chopped red onion to the grated potatoes for extra flavour and colour.

6 Lift the hash browns out of the pan with a fish slice and drain on a plate lined with kitchen paper. Serve hot.

SERVES 4

BOILING, STEAMING AND POACHING

Boiling, steaming and poaching are all done on the hob and, just like when you are frying, it's important to use the right size and shape of pan.

TYPES OF PAN

FOR BOILING

A straight-sided saucepan with a tight-fitting lid is used for boiling, the size of the pan depending on the quantity of ingredients you are cooking. However, pasta should always be boiled in a large pan so the strands or shapes have plenty of room to cook evenly and don't stick together.

FOR POACHING

A wide, shallow pan such as a sauté pan is best for poaching eggs. Eggs can be poached by cracking them directly into a pan of simmering – rather than fast boiling – water, or you can use special poaching cups that are lowered into the water and help the eggs keep their shape as they cook.

FOR STEAMING

Steaming can be done in either a metal colander or steaming basket on top of a conventional saucepan that is covered with a tight-fitting lid.

WATCH OUT

Always take extra care when cooking with hot or boiling water. Protect your hands with oven gloves as, just like hot water, steam can cause painful burns.

Technique 1: BOILING PASTA

Different types of pasta, such as spaghetti, penne and pasta bows, require different cooking times, so always check the instructions on the packet. Most dried pastas take around 10 minutes to cook, while fresh pastas only need a couple of minutes. Allow 100–125 g (3½–4 oz) of dried pasta per person and 150–175 g (5–6 oz) of fresh pasta.

give it a stir!

1 Fill a large saucepan about two-thirds full with cold water. Place it on the hob and bring the water to a fast boil. Add half a teaspoon of salt.

2 Carefully add the pasta to the water. If it is a short-cut pasta such as penne, you can do this using a large spoon. If it's a long pasta, hold the bundle of pasta upright at one end and lower the other end into the water. Bend the pasta round as the part that is in the water starts to soften, so the remaining pasta can be pushed gently into the water.

3 Boil for the length of time recommended on the packet, stirring occasionally to make sure the pasta is not sticking to the bottom of the pan.

4 To see if the pasta is ready, carefully lift out one piece with a fork and let it cool for a few moments before biting into it. The pasta should be tender but not too soft and still have a little bite – what Italians call 'al dente'.

5 Put a large colander in the sink and drain the pasta into this.

Technique 2: STEAMING VEGETABLES

Vegetables such as broccoli, cauliflower, new potatoes, baby carrots and peas are best steamed rather than boiled, as the steam cooks the vegetables just as quickly as boiling but none of their flavour is lost in the water. Take care when you lift the lid of the steamer to check if the vegetables are cooked, as hot steam will escape and could burn you.

TAKE CARE!

1 Prepare vegetables as necessary by peeling off their skins, trimming tough stalks or removing peas or broad beans from their pods.

2 Slice or chop the vegetables into bite-sized pieces, dividing cauliflower and broccoli into small florets.

3 Half-fill a saucepan with cold water, place on the hob and bring the water to the boil.

4 Put your vegetables into a steaming basket or colander and place this on top of the saucepan. Cover with a tight-fitting lid.

5 Cook for 5–10 minutes or until the vegetables are just tender. Pierce with a skewer or the point of a knife to check if they're ready.

Technique 3: POACHING EGGS

Poached eggs are delicious served on hot buttered English muffins. You need to use a large pan: either a sauté pan or large saucepan. The fresher the eggs, the less they will spread when they're put into the water

1 Half-fill a large pan with cold water, add 2 tablespoons of vinegar and heat on the hob until the water comes to a simmer – small bubbles will appear over the surface.

2 While the water is heating, crack a fresh egg into a cup.

3 When the water reaches the right temperature, swirl it with a large spoon and slide the egg out of the cup and into the water. The swirling water will make the egg white curl and wrap itself around the yolk.

4 Leave to cook for 3–4 minutes, depending on how set you want the egg yolk to be. Carefully lift the egg from the water using a slotted spoon or a fish slice and drain on a plate lined with kitchen paper.

USING A POACHING CUP

1 Eggs can also be poached in special poaching cups. Lightly grease the cups with oil and crack an egg into each.

2 Lower the cups into a shallow pan of simmering water. Cover the pan with a lid and leave until the eggs are cooked.

3 Protecting your hand with an oven glove, lift out the cups with a fish slice before scooping out the poached eggs.

mmm... tasty!

EGGS BENEDICT

YOU WILL NEED

Bread knife

Large plate lined with kitchen paper

Large spoon

Large saucepan or sauté pan

Small bowl

Slotted spoon or fish slice

Butter knife

Ham and poached eggs on toasted English muffins, topped with creamy hollandaise sauce, is a brunch that all the family will love. Make it for your mum on Mother's Day for extra brownie points!

INGREDIENTS

- 4 large eggs
- 2 English muffins
- 8 tbsp hollandaise sauce
- 40 g (1½ oz) butter
- 8 thin slices of ham

1 Follow the technique for poaching an egg in a poaching cup (see page 37) cooking all four eggs together in the pan over a gentle heat for 3-4 minutes.

2 While the eggs are cooking, split the muffins in half and toast them. Microwave the hollandaise sauce in a small bowl on low power for about 1 minute until warm but not bubbling.

CHECK YOUR SKILLS

- p. 42 for grilling
- p. 37 for poaching eggs

3 Spread butter on the cut sides of the muffins and put them on serving plates. Arrange the ham slices on top.

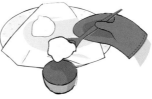

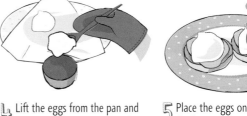

4 Lift the eggs from the pan and drain briefly on a plate lined with kitchen paper to absorb any water on the eggs.

5 Place the eggs on top of the ham and spoon the hollandaise sauce over the eggs. Serve at once.

QUICK TIP... Jars of readymade hollandaise sauce are easy to find in supermarkets.

TRY THIS!

For a vegetarian version of Eggs Benedict, replace the slices of ham with cooked spinach. Rinse and chop fresh spinach leaves – about 50g (2oz) per person – put them in a microwaveable bowl and cook for 2 minutes until the leaves have wilted.

SERVES 4

Breakfast is served!

PERFECT PASTA *with a* Creamy Mushroom Sauce

You can serve this mushroom sauce with any type of pasta – spaghetti, linguine, tagliatelle or a short pasta such as shells or bows would all be equally good.

YOU WILL NEED

Cook's knife
Chopping board
Large saucepan
Colander
Sauté pan
Small bowl
Spoon

INGREDIENTS

- 2 tbsp olive oil or sunflower oil
- 1 red onion, peeled and thinly sliced
- 225 g (8 oz) button mushrooms, quartered
- 300 ml (½pt) chicken or vegetable stock, made from a stock cube
- 400–450 g (14 oz–1 lb) spaghetti, or other dried pasta
- 1 tsp cornflour
- 4 tbsp soured cream or natural yoghurt

TO SERVE:
- Grated Parmesan cheese

CHECK YOUR SKILLS

- p. 7 for slicing onions
- p. 13 for grating cheese
- p. 31 for sautéing
- p. 36 for boiling pasta

SERVES 4

1 Heat the oil in a sauté pan, add the onion and cover the pan. Cook for 5 minutes or until the onion has started to soften. Take the lid off the pan, add the mushrooms and cook for a further 5 minutes, stirring occasionally.

2 Add the stock and leave to simmer over a low heat with the lid on the pan. While this is simmering, cook the spaghetti, following the instructions on the packet.

QUICK TIP... Before you quarter the mushrooms, put them in a colander and run cold water over them to rinse them. Pat the mushrooms dry with kitchen paper.

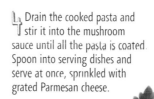

4 Drain the cooked pasta and stir it into the mushroom sauce until all the pasta is coated. Spoon into serving dishes and serve at once, sprinkled with grated Parmesan cheese.

3 In a small bowl, stir the cornflour into the soured cream or yoghurt and add to the pan. Stir until evenly blended in, bring back to a simmer and cook for a further 2 minutes.

TRY THIS! Instead of pasta, serve the delicious sauce spooned over roast chicken legs.

STEAMED ASIAN DUMPLINGS

Time to practise your chopstick skills! For a Chinese feast, serve these little dumplings with the Vegetable Fried Rice on page 41.

YOU WILL NEED

Steamer
Cook's knife
Chopping board
Teaspoon
Pastry brush
Mixing bowl

INGREDIENTS

- 175 g (6 oz) minced chicken or pork
- 75 g (3 oz) cooked prawns, finely chopped
- 2 salad onions, finely chopped
- 2 tsp fresh ginger, peeled and very finely chopped (or 1 tsp shop-bought ginger purée)
- 2 tbsp soy sauce
- 5 water chestnuts, from a can, drained and finely chopped
- 30 wonton wrappers
- 1 egg white, lightly whisked

TO SERVE:
- Soy sauce, for dipping

CHECK YOUR SKILLS

- p. 7 for chopping
- p. 37 for steaming

1 Put the minced chicken or pork in a bowl and stir in the chopped prawns, salad onions, ginger, soy sauce and chopped water chestnuts.

2 Lay a wonton wrapper on a chopping board and spoon 1 teaspoon of the mixture in the centre.

QUICK TIP... If you find you have some filling left, make a few more wontons rather than add extra filling to the ones already completed. If the wrappers are over-filled, they could burst or split when steamed.

3 Brush the edges of the wrapper with egg white and gather them up around the filling to enclose it. Pinch the edges of the wrapper together at the top to seal it. Repeat with the remaining wrappers and filling.

4 Arrange the dumplings in a Chinese or other steamer without them touching – you may need to cook them in batches – and steam for 5 minutes.

5 Serve the dumplings hot with a bowl of extra soy sauce for dipping.

MAKES ABOUT 30

TRY THIS!
You can vary the filling for the dumplings by adding different ingredients. Try chopped mushrooms or red pepper instead of prawns and a chopped shallot instead of salad onions. If you like garlic, you can stir in a couple of crushed cloves. Just remember to chop everything as finely as you can.

VEGETABLE FRIED RICE

Fried rice is a great Chinese favourite and you can switch it up by adding different vegetables, prawns, pork or chicken. Whatever you add, take care to chop all the ingredients into small, similar-sized pieces so they cook evenly.

INGREDIENTS

- 350 g (12 oz) long grain rice
- ½ tsp salt
- 2 tbsp groundnut or sunflower oil
- ½ red pepper, deseeded and finely chopped
- ½ green pepper, deseeded and finely chopped
- 125 g (4 oz) chestnut mushrooms, thinly sliced
- 125 g (4 oz) sweetcorn kernels
- 125 g (4 oz) frozen peas
- 4 salad onions, finely chopped
- 2 large eggs, beaten
- 2 tbsp oyster sauce or light soy sauce

YOU WILL NEED

Sieve

Saucepan with a lid

Wok or large frying pan

Metal spatula or large spoon

Fork

1 Put the rice into a sieve and run cold water over it until the water is clear.

2 Tip the rice into a saucepan and add 700 ml (23 fl oz) cold water and the salt. Stir once, then bring to the boil. Turn the heat down as low as it will go and cover the pan with a lid. Cook the rice for 10–15 minutes without taking the lid off the pan, until the rice is tender and has absorbed the water.

CHECK YOUR SKILLS

- p. 6 for using knives
- p. 36 for boiling
- p. 30 for stir-frying

QUICK TIP... It's not necessary to thaw the frozen peas before you add them. They'll soon defrost when mixed with the other hot vegetables.

3 Heat the oil in a wok or large frying pan and, using a metal spatula or large spoon, stir-fry the red and green peppers over a fairly high heat for 3 minutes. Add the mushrooms and stir-fry for 2 minutes.

4 Add the sweetcorn, frozen peas and salad onions, and stir-fry for 2 minutes. Push the vegetables to one side of the pan and pour in the eggs. Leave until they start to set, then scramble them by stirring with a fork.

5 Mix the egg with the vegetables and add the rice and oyster or soy sauce. Toss everything together over the heat for 2 minutes, spoon into serving bowls and serve at once.

SERVES 2-4

GRILLING, ROASTING AND BAKING

Grilling is a quick way of cooking small cuts of meat or fish, while roasting involves longer, slower cooking of larger joints of meat or vegetables in the oven. Baking is the word used for cooking bread, cakes, pastry and cookies in the oven – in fact, everything that you'd buy in a baker's shop!

EQUIPMENT NEEDED

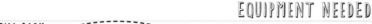

GRILL RACK
This can be a rack that fits into a grill pan of the same size supplied with an oven or the rack of a barbecue.

BAKING TIN
Similar to a baking sheet but with very shallow sides. Used for making Swiss rolls and tray bakes.

ROASTING TIN
A large rectangular tin with shallow, straight sides used for roasting poultry, joints of meat and vegetables.

DEEP CAKE TINS
These are used for making large cakes and are usually round or square. The tins are around 7.5 cm deep.

BAKING SHEET
A flat metal sheet used for baking meringues, cookies and scones. As the sheet has no sides, it is easy to slide the baked items off it directly onto a cooling rack.

SANDWICH TINS
These round cake tins are usually 4 cm deep. They are used for baking layers of sponge to be sandwiched with jam, whipped cream or buttercream frosting.

Technique 1: SETTING UP THE GRILL TRAY

Grilling is done by placing food on an open wire rack with a high heat coming either from above, if using a conventional kitchen grill, or below, if using a barbecue.

1 For a kitchen grill, fit the rack into its tray and attach the handle to the tray if one is provided. You can line the grill rack with foil if you want to spoon any juices that run out over the food as it cooks.

Optional: line the grill with foil to catch the juices.

2 Heat up the grill. If you're using a gas grill, you can adjust the flames according to the level of heat you need. If you're using an electric grill, you'll need to position the tray close to the heat if you want the food to cook very quickly, but lower it down if, once browned, the food needs to cook more slowly.

3 Place your steaks, burgers, kebabs or whatever you are cooking on the grill rack in a single layer.

4 Grill one side of the food until it is well browned, but watch it carefully to make sure it doesn't burn. Then turn it over with tongs to cook the other side.

Technique 2: USING BAKING PARCHMENT

Baking parchment is a special kitchen paper that has a silicone coating to prevent baked items such as cookies, cakes and meringues from sticking to baking sheets or cake tins. Both sides of the parchment are non-stick, which means there is no right or wrong way up to use it.

overlap and cut the string

1 To line a baking sheet, brush the sheet lightly with a flavourless oil such as sunflower or groundnut. Cut a piece of baking parchment slightly smaller than the size of the sheet and lay this on top, smoothing it out evenly – the oil stops the parchment sliding around.

2 To line a deep, round cake tin, place the tin on a sheet of baking parchment and draw around the base. Using kitchen scissors, cut round just inside the drawn line.

3 Measure the circumference of the tin by wrapping a length of string around the sides and snipping the string so it is 2.5 cm longer. Cut a strip of parchment the same length as the string and 5 cm deeper than the tin.

4 Fold over the bottom 2.5 cm of the strip, open the fold and make cuts with scissors as deep as the crease you have just made, about 2.5 cm apart.

5 Brush the inside of the tin lightly with oil. Take the long strip of parchment and angle it into the tin with the cuts at the bottom. Make sure it sticks smoothly around the sides with no creases and the cuts lie flat around the bottom of the tin.

6 Slide the round piece of parchment into the tin to cover the base, laying it over the cut sections at the bottom.

Technique 3: ROASTING A CHICKEN IN FOIL

Covering a chicken with foil for the first part of the roasting time ensures the flesh cooks evenly and doesn't dry out.

BE CAREFUL WHEN REMOVING THE FOIL FROM THE CHICKEN AS HOT STEAM CAN GIVE NASTY BURNS.

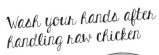
Wash your hands after handling raw chicken

1 Weigh the chicken to calculate the total roasting time, allowing 25 minutes per 450 g (1 lb) plus a further 25 minutes.

2 Stand the chicken in a roasting tin and cover it loosely with a sheet of foil. Tuck the foil under the rim of the roasting tin to secure it in place and make sure the foil forms a 'tent' over the chicken and isn't sticking to the skin.

3 Preheat the oven to 200°C/400°F/gas 6 and roast the chicken for the calculated time, carefully removing the foil for the final 25 minutes so the skin becomes brown and crisp.

4 To check the chicken is fully cooked, push a skewer into the thickest part of one of the legs – the juices that run out should be clear and not pink. Turn off the oven and leave the chicken inside for 10 minutes to rest before serving.

DON'T FORGET TO WEAR OVEN GLOVES WHEN TAKING ANYTHING OUT OF A HOT OVEN.

MINI PITTA PIZZAS

These mini pizzas are the perfect after-school snack – quick and easy to make and great fun to eat. You can try out the toppings in this recipe, or add any others you like.

YOU WILL NEED

Cook's knife

Chopping board

Spoon or round-bladed knife to spread the tomato purée

Pastry brush

Grater, if grating the mozzarella

INGREDIENTS

- 8 mini pitta breads
- 4 tbsp tomato purée
- 4 chestnut mushrooms, sliced
- ½ green pepper, deseeded and cut into thin slices
- 2 tomatoes, sliced
- 2 tbsp extra virgin olive oil
- 2 tsp dried oregano or mixed herbs
- 100 g (3½ oz) mozzarella cheese, grated or sliced

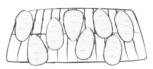

1 Arrange the pitta breads on the grill rack in a single layer.

2 Spread the tomato purée over them to within 1 cm of the edge of the pittas.

CHECK YOUR SKILLS

- p. 6 for slicing tomatoes
- p. 13 for using graters
- p. 42 for grilling

3 Top with the mushroom, green pepper and tomato slices, dividing them evenly.

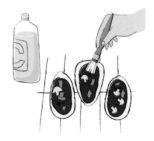

4 Brush the vegetables with the olive oil and sprinkle over the herbs.

5 Top with the grated or sliced mozzarella and grill until the cheese melts. Serve at once.

Finger food!

SERVES 4

TRY THIS!
Pepperoni, chopped ham, corn kernels, red onion slices and salami all make great pizza toppings. You can use grated Cheddar cheese instead of mozzarella if you prefer.

QUICK TIP... You can make as many or as few pitta pizzas as you like. All you need to do is use less or more of the topping ingredients. You'll quickly get the hang of how much you need to make one or two pizzas.

CHICKEN SATAY

These spicy chicken kebabs are grilled on open-air barbecues in Thailand and Malaysia, where they are enjoyed as quick and tasty street food. You can cook them under your kitchen grill, or outdoors on a barbecue when the weather is hot.

INGREDIENTS

FOR THE CHICKEN SATAY:

- 4 boneless chicken breasts, skinned
- 2.5 cm (1 in) piece of root ginger, peeled and grated or finely chopped
- 2 cloves of garlic, peeled and crushed
- 2 tbsp brown sugar
- Juice of 1 lime
- 2 tbsp soy sauce
- 2 tsp groundnut or vegetable oil, plus extra for brushing

FOR THE PEANUT SAUCE:

- 1 small onion, peeled and finely chopped
- 1 tbsp groundnut or vegetable oil
- 1 tsp chilli sauce
- 2 tbsp soy sauce
- 175 g (6 oz) peanut butter, smooth or crunchy
- Juice of 1 lime
- 150 ml (¼ pt) water

YOU WILL NEED

Cook's knife
Chopping board
Cling film
12 metal or wooden skewers
Pastry brush
Tongs
Small bowl
Large spoon
Small saucepan
Large bowl

1 To make the chicken satay, cut the chicken into thin strips across the breasts and place in a bowl or shallow dish.

2 Mix together the ginger, garlic, brown sugar, lime juice, soy sauce and oil in a small bowl and pour over the chicken. Cover the bowl with cling film and leave the chicken to marinate for 1 hour or longer.

CHECK YOUR SKILLS

- p. 7 for chopping onions
- p.19 for juicing
- p. 31 for frying onions
- p. 42 for using the grill

3 Lift out the chicken and thread the pieces onto the skewers to make 'S' shapes. Brush with oil and lay side by side on the grill rack. Grill for 5 minutes, using tongs to turn the skewers over once or twice.

4 To make the sauce, fry the onion in the oil in a small saucepan until it is soft and golden brown. Add the rest of the ingredients and stir constantly over a low heat for 2 minutes until hot and all the ingredients are evenly mixed. Serve the chicken kebabs with the warm sauce.

SERVES 4-6

QUICK TIP... You can use either metal or wooden skewers, but don't forget to soak wooden skewers in water for 30 minutes first or cover the ends with foil, so they don't burn under the grill.

CHOCOLATE CHIP COOKIES

Soft and chewy in the middle, crisp on the outside and studded with chocolate chips – it's not surprising these cookies are everyone's favourite. They won't hang around in the cookie jar for long!

YOU WILL NEED

- 2 baking sheets
- Wire cooling rack
- Wooden spoon or electric whisk
- Large metal spoon
- Palette knife
- Sieve
- Mixing bowl
- Baking parchment

INGREDIENTS

- A little groundnut or sunflower oil, for greasing
- 150 g (5 oz) butter, cut into small pieces and softened
- 75 g (3 oz) light soft brown sugar
- 75 g (3 oz) caster sugar
- 1 large egg
- 1 tsp vanilla extract
- 200 g (7 oz) dark chocolate chips
- 225 g (8 oz) self-raising flour

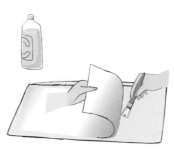

1 Preheat the oven to 190°C/375°F/gas 5. Brush two baking sheets lightly with oil and line with baking parchment.

2 Beat the butter and sugar together in a mixing bowl until light and fluffy. Beat in the egg and vanilla extract and then stir in the chocolate chips.

CHECK YOUR SKILLS

- p. 52 for beating butter and sugar together
- p. 43 for baking

3 Sieve in the flour and stir it in with a large metal spoon until all the ingredients are evenly mixed.

4 Place 12 small mounds of mixture onto each baking sheet, leaving plenty of space between each one as the cookies will spread when they bake. Make each into a round shape and flatten slightly on top with the back of the spoon.

5 Bake for about 10 minutes or until the cookies are golden. Allow to cool on the baking sheets for 5 minutes before lifting them off with a palette knife and transferring to a wire rack to cool completely.

MAKES 24 COOKIES

QUICK TIP... The cookies are ready to come out of the oven when that are starting to brown at the edges but are still a little soft in the centre.

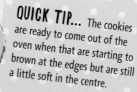

TRY THIS! For some really indulgent cookies, use a mixture of white, milk and dark chocolate chips.

ROASTED MEDITERRANEAN
Vegetables

Think you're not a fan of veg? Well, think again! This colourful mix of roasted vegetables will be a holiday for your taste buds! It's great as a side dish for pork chops or chicken legs.

YOU WILL NEED

Measuring spoons

Cook's knife

Chopping board

Mixing bowl

Large spoon

Roasting tin

INGREDIENTS

- 4 tbsp olive oil
- 1 red onion, peeled and cut into wedges
- 1 each red, orange and yellow peppers, halved, seeds removed and cut into 2.5 cm pieces
- 100 g (3½ oz) mushrooms, halved or quartered
- 2 medium courgettes, ends trimmed off and thickly sliced
- 1 small aubergine, stalk removed and cut into 2.5 cm pieces
- 1 tbsp balsamic or white wine vinegar

1 Measure 3 tablespoons of the olive oil into a large bowl and add the onion wedges, pepper pieces, mushrooms, courgettes and aubergine chunks. Stir well until the vegetables are coated in the oil.

2 Preheat the oven to 200°C/ 400°F/gas 6. Spoon the vegetables into a roasting tin and spread them out in an even layer.

CHECK YOUR SKILLS

- p. 6–7 for preparing vegetables
- p. 42–43 for roasting

3 Roast the vegetables in the oven for 35–40 minutes or until they are tender and browned at the edges.

4 Mix together the remaining tablespoon of olive oil with the vinegar. Take the vegetables out of the oven and drizzle the mixture over them.

TRY THIS!

Halloumi is a semi-hard cheese from Cyprus that can be heated to quite a high temperature without melting. Cut a halloumi cheese into 5 mm slices and cook the slices in a hot griddle pan for 1–2 minutes on each side until scorched with brown lines. Serve the hot cheese slices with the vegetables.

SERVES 4–6

5 Spoon the vegetables into a serving dish and serve hot or leave to cool before serving.

Lip-smackingly good

MAKING SWEET AND SAVOURY SAUCES

Nobody wants a lumpy sauce to spoil their cooking. From making a smooth and creamy sauce to add to a savoury dish, to jazzing up a dessert with a homemade coulis, there will be no stopping you once you have the knack.

EQUIPMENT NEEDED

MILK PAN
This saucepan has one or two pouring lips to prevent milk or other hot liquids spilling when you pour them out of the pan.

MEASURING JUG
You'll need this to measure the exact quantity of liquid you need for making a sauce.

WIRE SIEVE
A fine mesh sieve with a handle is used to sieve the pips and seeds out of a fruit coulis.

SAUCEPAN AND HEATPROOF BOWL
Chocolate will spoil if it gets too hot, so it's best to melt it in a heatproof bowl on top of a saucepan.

FLAT WHISK
This type of whisk can reach into the corners of a saucepan to stop lumps of flour collecting there and making your sauce lumpy.

Technique 1: MAKING CHOCOLATE SAUCE

You can drizzle chocolate sauce over all sorts of desserts to make them that little bit more special – vanilla ice cream, plain sponge cake, brownies, cheesecakes, or fresh fruit – you name it! The sauce can be served warm or cold.

Make sure you use a heat-proof bowl.

1 Chop 300 g (11 oz) of dark chocolate or break it into small pieces.

2 Place the chocolate in a heatproof bowl and add 175ml (6 fl oz) of double cream, 2 tablespoons of golden syrup and 15 g (½ oz) of butter.

3 Put a saucepan, one-third filled with water, on the hob and bring the water to a gentle simmer.

4 Stand the bowl on top of the saucepan, making sure the bottom of the bowl does not touch the water. Leave it there until the chocolate, golden syrup and butter have melted, stirring occasionally until you have a smooth sauce.

5 Serve the chocolate sauce straight away while it is still warm or leave it to cool, stirring occasionally.

GENTLY DOES IT
If chocolate gets too hot as it melts, it will develop an unattractive, grainy texture, so make sure the bottom of the bowl is above the water and do not let the water in the saucepan bubble hard. It should only be simmering gently.

The bowl should form a tight seal with the top of the pan. This is so that no steam can escape from the pan and cause moisture to come into contact with the melting mixture in the bowl.

Technique 2: MAKING A WHITE SAUCE

A plain white sauce can be flavoured with different ingredients such as grated cheese, chopped parsley or sliced mushrooms. Cheese sauce is the most popular white sauce, since it can be used in many different dishes. It's particularly tasty in baked pasta dishes such as lasagne, cannelloni or macaroni cheese (page 51).

1 To make a white sauce to serve 4 people, melt 25 g (1 oz) of butter in a saucepan on the hob over a low heat. When the butter has melted, take the saucepan off the heat and stir in 25 g (1 oz) of plain flour or cornflour to make a smooth mixture – this is called a 'roux'.

2 Put the saucepan back on a low heat and cook the roux gently for 2 minutes so that it bubbles gently but does not change colour.

3 Remove the pan from the heat again and gradually stir in 300 ml (½ pt) of milk. Keep stirring until the mixture is smooth and there are no lumps.

4 Put the pan back on the hob and turn up the heat to medium. Bring the sauce to the boil, stirring continuously, until it is thickened, glossy and smooth. Cook for a further 1 minute.

5 Season the sauce with a little salt and some freshly ground white pepper. Stir in grated cheese or other flavourings off the heat.

WATCH OUT FOR LUMPS!
Use a wooden spoon or – even better – a flat sauce whisk to get right into the corners of the pan. You must stir the sauce constantly as it comes to the boil. If any lumps form, take the pan off the heat and beat the sauce as vigorously as you can. Once the sauce has boiled, the only way to get rid of lumps is to use a handheld or goblet blender.

Technique 3: MAKING A FRUIT COULIS

A coulis is a sweet, smooth fruit sauce that is made by simmering fresh or dried fruit in water or another liquid, such as fruit juice, until the fruit is soft. The fruit and liquid is then blended together to make a smooth purée, using a food processor or handheld blender. If necessary, it is then sieved to remove any skin or seeds. Fruit that is already soft, such as raspberries or strawberries, doesn't need to be cooked first. It can simply be puréed, sieved and then thinned to the right consistency with cold water or fruit juice.

1 To make a strawberry coulis to serve 4 people, remove the hulls from 250 g (9 oz) of ripe strawberries.

2 Put the strawberries in a goblet blender (or use a bowl and a handheld blender), add 100ml (3½ fl oz) of apple or orange juice or cold water and 25 g (1 oz) of icing sugar.

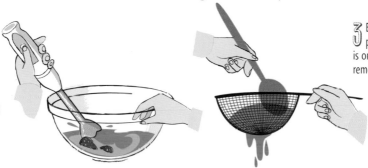

3 Blend until you have a smooth purée and serve the coulis as it is or push it through a sieve to remove the seeds.

4 Taste the coulis after you've made it and adjust the sweetness by stirring in a little extra icing sugar or a spoonful of honey, if needed.

APRICOT COULIS with Yoghurt and Toasted Oats

YOU WILL NEED

Saucepan with a lid

Handheld blender, goblet blender or food processor

Spoon

Frying pan

6 tumblers

This recipe is fun if you want something a bit different for breakfast, and it also makes a lovely dessert. Spoon the ingredients into tumblers or other glasses so you can see the colourful layers.

INGREDIENTS

- 225 g (8 oz) ready-to-eat dried apricots
- 300 ml (½ pt) fresh orange juice
- 25 g (1 oz) butter
- 50 g (2 oz) porridge oats
- 40 g (1½ oz) chopped hazelnuts
- 2 tbsp light soft brown sugar
- 2 tbsp clear honey
- 250 g (9 oz) thick natural yoghurt

1 Put the apricots in a saucepan and pour over the orange juice. Put a lid on the pan and simmer the apricots for 15 minutes until they are soft.

2 Leave the apricots to cool and then blend the contents of the pan to a smooth purée.

CHECK YOUR SKILLS

- p. 49 for making a fruit coulis

SERVES 6

3 Melt the butter in a frying pan, add the oats and hazelnuts and spread them out with the back of the spoon. Cook for 1–2 minutes until the oats and nuts are lightly toasted, stirring frequently.

4 Sprinkle the brown sugar into the pan of oats and nuts and cook for a further 1 minute. Remove from the heat and leave to cool.

5 Stir the honey into the yoghurt until evenly mixed in.

Yum yum!

QUICK TIP... Instead of using only apricots, you could make the coulis with 175 g (6 oz) apricots and 1 apple, peeled, cored and chopped, cooking and then blending the two fruits together with the orange juice.

6 Layer up the apricot purée with the yoghurt and the oat mixture in six tumblers, finishing with a sprinkling of the oat mixture on the top of each one. Chill until ready to serve.

MACARONI CHEESE *with* Cherry Tomatoes

Mac 'n' Cheese will always be a family favourite as long as the cook uses plenty of rich cheese to coat the macaroni. Including cherry tomatoes in the mix doesn't just add extra flavour; the vibrant red tomatoes make it look good, too.

YOU WILL NEED

Large spoon   *Grater*

Large saucepan   *Measuring jug*

Large ovenproof dish

INGREDIENTS

- 250 g (9 oz) macaroni
- 40 g (1½ oz) butter
- 40 g (1½ oz) plain flour
- 600 ml (1 pt) milk
- 225 g (8 oz) strong mature Cheddar cheese, grated
- 175 g (6 oz) cherry tomatoes, halved
- 50 g (2 oz) grated Parmesan cheese

1 Cook the macaroni in a large saucepan of boiling water according to the packet instructions. Drain and set aside.

2 Heat the butter in the saucepan over a low heat until it melts.

CHECK YOUR SKILLS

- p. 12 for grating
- p.36 for boiling pasta
- p. 49 for making a white sauce

3 Take the pan off the heat and stir in the flour until you have a smooth mixture. Cook this gently so it bubbles over a low heat for 2 minutes.

4 Remove the pan from the heat and gradually stir in the milk until the mixture is completely smooth. Put the pan back over a medium heat and bring to the boil, stirring all the time to prevent any lumps forming in your sauce. Simmer for 1 minute.

5 Stir the macaroni, 175 g (6 oz) of the Cheddar cheese and the halved tomatoes into the sauce and spoon the mixture into an ovenproof dish. Sprinkle the rest of the Cheddar and the Parmesan over the top.

6 Preheat the oven to 200°C/ 400°F/gas 6 and bake for 30 minutes or until until bubbling hot and golden and crusty on top. Serve at once.

QUICK TIP... If you think your sauce is in danger of becoming lumpy, take the saucepan off the heat and stir or whisk until it is smooth again before continuing. If the sauce looks like it is about to bubble over, take the pan off the heat, and turn the heat down before putting the pan back on.

SERVES 4

BEATING, WHIPPING AND WHISKING

Beating, whipping and whisking are all slightly different, depending on what equipment and ingredients you use. They are important skills to master, as you'll use them for lots of recipes.

BEATING
This usually applies to mixtures that contain whole eggs such as cake batters, puddings and choux pastry. You 'beat' to mix ingredients together until everything is evenly combined. Beating is also used to make flavoured butters.

WHIPPING
Whipping is done with a whisk to add air to a mixture, changing its texture increasing its volume. It usually applies to cream, which is whipped until thickened enough to hold its shape.

WHISKING
Technically this is the same as whipping, but the difference is that cream is 'whipped' but whole eggs or egg whites are 'whisked' to make omelettes and meringues.

EQUIPMENT NEEDED

WOODEN SPOON
Ideal for beating a mixture until smooth.

BALLOON WHISK
Easy to use and great for whipping air into a mixture.

ELECTRIC WHISK
A quick way to mix ingredients. The blades are easy to remove for cleaning.

Technique 1: BEATING BUTTER AND SUGAR TOGETHER

This technique is used when making sponge cakes and buttercream frostings. It involves beating the measured butter and sugar together until they are pale in colour and fluffy. Not only does it mix the butter and sugar evenly, it also beats in air so the baked cake or buttercream frosting has a beautifully light texture.

1 Take the butter out of the fridge about 30 minutes before you need it. Measure the amount you need and return the rest to the fridge. Cut your butter into small pieces and leave to soften.

2 Put the butter in a mixing bowl and beat it with a wooden spoon or electric handheld whisk until it is smooth.

3 Add the sugar to the beaten butter.

4 Beat the sugar and butter together until they combine to make a light, fluffy mixture that is pale in colour.

Technique 2: WHIPPING CREAM

You can whip cream for adding to desserts, cakes or even topping a bowl of soup. Use double cream or whipping cream, but not single cream, as this won't thicken up when whipped.

stir the whisk in circles

1 Pour your double or whipping cream into a mixing bowl.

2 Using a balloon whisk in a circular motion, whip the cream until it stands in soft peaks that hold their shape.

3 Alternatively, whip the cream using a handheld electric whisk set on medium speed. As soon as the cream starts to thicken, reduce the speed to low and continue until the cream holds its shape.

4 If you over-whip cream it will become grainy and start to separate. If this happens, stir in 1–2 tablespoons of cold milk until the cream stands in soft peaks again.

Technique 3: WHISKING EGG WHITES

Egg whites must be whisked in a clean mixing bowl as any grease sticking to the sides of the bowl will prevent the whites whisking up. As yolks contain fat, take care that none gets into the whites before you whisk them.

1 Take your eggs out of the fridge about 30 minutes before you need them so they have time to come to room temperature – this will make the whites easier to whisk.

2 Tap the egg on the side of a clean, dry bowl, and carefully pull the shell apart. Tip the egg onto a small plate or saucer.

3 Place one half of the shell over the yolk and tilt the plate so just the white slides off into the bowl. Repeat with the rest of the eggs.

4 Whisk the egg whites using a balloon whisk or handheld electric whisk on medium speed until the whites stand in soft or stiff peaks, depending on the recipe you are making.

CHOCOLATE *Sponge Cake*

You could make this cake to celebrate a birthday and decorate it for the person you're giving it to. Don't forget the candles!

YOU WILL NEED

Wire cooling rack

Sieve

Mixing bowl

Wooden spoon or electric handheld whisk

Pastry brush

Measuring spoons

Palette knife

Large spoon

Two 20 cm sandwich tins

Baking parchment

CHECK YOUR SKILLS

- p. 52 for beating
- p. 48 for melting chocolate
- p. 42–43 for using the oven

INGREDIENTS

FOR THE CAKE MIXTURE:
- 175 g (6 oz) butter, cut into small pieces and softened
- 175 g (6 oz) light soft brown sugar
- 3 large eggs
- 175 g (6 oz) plain flour
- 1 ½ tbsp cocoa powder
- 1 ½ tsp baking powder

TO FILL AND FROST THE CAKE:
- 150 g (5 oz) butter, cut into small pieces and softened
- 275 g (9½ oz) icing sugar, sieved
- 50 g (2 oz) dark chocolate, melted
- 1 tbsp cocoa powder
- 1 tbsp milk

Squelch

SERVES 8–10

1 Preheat the oven to 180°C/ 350°F/gas 4. Line the bases of your sandwich tins with parchment.

2 Beat the butter in a mixing bowl until smooth and then beat in the brown sugar until light and fluffy.

5 Divide the mixture between the sandwich tins, spreading the tops level, and bake for 25–30 minutes. Push a cocktail stick into the centre of each cake layer: it's ready if it comes out clean.

6 Cool the cakes in the tins for 15 minutes before turning out onto a wire rack to cool completely. Peel off the lining paper.

QUICK TIP... As sandwich tins are shallower than ordinary cake tins, you only need to line the bases with baking parchment. Some tins also have loose bottoms, which makes it much easier to turn out the cakes.

3 Beat in the eggs one at a time, adding a tablespoon of the flour with each egg to stop the mixture curdling.

4 Sieve in the rest of the flour with the cocoa powder and baking powder, and stir until mixed in.

7 To make the buttercream frosting, beat the butter until smooth. Gradually beat in the icing sugar and, when it has all been added, beat in the melted chocolate, cocoa powder, and milk.

8 Sandwich the cake layers together with some of the buttercream frosting and spread the rest evenly over the top and sides with a palette knife.

STRAWBERRY *Pavlova*

A pavlova doesn't just taste gorgeous, it looks impressive too. You can top it with strawberries or other fruits such as raspberries, mango, or kiwi fruit.

INGREDIENTS

- 3 egg whites
- 175 g (6 oz) caster or icing sugar
- 1 tsp vinegar
- 1 tsp cornflour
- Oil for brushing

FOR THE FILLING:
- 300 ml (½ pt) double cream, whipped
- 350 g (12 oz) strawberries, halved if large

YOU WILL NEED

Baking parchment
Baking sheet
Large mixing bowl
Balloon whisk or handheld electric whisk
Metal tablespoon
Fish slice

1 Preheat the oven to 150°C/ 300°F/gas 2. Using a plate as a guide, draw a 20 cm circle on a sheet of baking parchment. Turn the parchment over and place it on a lightly greased baking sheet.

2 Put the egg whites in a large mixing bowl that is clean and dry. Using a balloon whisk or handheld electric whisk on medium speed, whisk the egg whites until they stand in soft peaks.

CHECK YOUR SKILLS

- p. 53 for whisking egg whites
- p. 53 for whipping cream
- p. 42–43 for using the oven

3 Begin adding the sugar 1 teaspoon at a time until the mixture starts to feel thicker, then whisk in the rest of the sugar in a slow, steady stream. Whisk in the vinegar and cornflour with the last of the sugar.

4 Spoon the meringue over the marked circle you have drawn on the baking parchment, making a slight hollow in the centre with the back of the spoon.

QUICK TIP... it is important to whisk the sugar in slowly so that it is absorbed by the egg whites.

Yummy!

SERVES 6

5 Bake the meringue for 1 hour or until it is crisp. Leave it to cool completely in the turned-off oven before carefully easing it off the parchment with a fish slice and placing it on a serving plate. A traditional meringue is crisp on the outside but chewy in the centre.

CHEESE OMELETTE

YOU WILL NEED

Omelette pan (a small frying pan with sloping sides, preferably non-stick)

Palette knife

Fork

Bowl

Grater

Omelettes make very popular brunch or lunch dishes. They're quick and easy, and you can add all sorts of ingredients to them, to keep even the fussiest eaters happy.

INGREDIENTS

- 2–3 eggs, depending on how hungry you are
- A little salt and freshly ground black pepper
- 15 g (½ oz) butter
- 50 g (2 oz) mature Cheddar cheese, grated

1 Crack the eggs into a bowl, add a little salt and some freshly ground black pepper and beat them with a fork until the yolks and whites are well mixed and the eggs are frothy.

2 Put the omelette pan on the hob over a medium heat. Add the butter and wait until it melts and foams.

CHECK YOUR SKILLS

- p. 13 for grating cheese
- p. 30 for frying

3 Pour in the beaten eggs and cook for about 30 seconds or until the eggs are lightly set on the bottom but still liquid on top.

4 As the eggs start to set, push the outer edges to the centre with a fork, so that the uncooked egg runs to the outside and cooks. Repeat this until the egg is cooked but still soft in the centre.

5 Sprinkle the grated cheese onto the centre of the omelette. Increase the heat to high and cook for about another 30 seconds so the omelette browns underneath and the cheese melts.

TRY THIS!

Here are some other delicious things you can add to an omelette:
- 1 slice of ham, chopped into small pieces
- 75 g (3 oz) sliced mushrooms, sautéed in olive oil first, until softened
- 2 bacon rashers or 1 large sausage, grilled and chopped into small pieces
- 1 tomato, diced, plus 2 fresh basil leaves, shredded.

SERVES 1

QUICK TIP... After you've added the butter to the pan, leave it until it melts and becomes foamy before pouring in the beaten eggs – don't leave it to go brown or it could spoil the flavour of your omelette.

6 Slide a palette knife around one side of the omelette and fold it over in half. Take the pan off the heat and tilt it slightly to one side so the folded omelette moves to the edge of the pan. Slide it out of the pan onto a warm plate and serve at once.

BANANA BREAD

Making a loaf of banana bread is a good way to use up over-ripe bananas – the ones still in the fruit bowl that nobody wants to eat! Over-ripe bananas are lovely and sweet and will give your banana bread a delicious flavour.

INGREDIENTS

- 250 g (9 oz) plain flour
- 2 tsp baking powder
- 1 tsp ground cinnamon
- 200 g (7 oz) light soft brown sugar
- 3–4 over-ripe bananas (total unpeeled weight about 350 g (12 oz))
- 2 eggs
- 200 ml (7fl oz) sunflower oil
- 50 g (2 oz) sultanas
- 50 g (2 oz) chopped walnuts or pecans

YOU WILL NEED

Sieve

900 g (2 lb) loaf tin, greased and lined with baking parchment

Mixing bowl   *Wooden spoon*

Goblet blender, handheld blender or food processor

Wire cooling rack

1 Preheat the oven to 180°C/350°F/gas 4. Sieve the flour, baking powder and cinnamon into a mixing bowl and stir in the sugar.

2 Peel the bananas and cut them into chunks. Liquidize the bananas, eggs and sunflower oil together and gradually beat into the dry ingredients.

CHECK YOUR SKILLS

- p. 25 for using a blender
- p. 52 for beating ingredients together

3 When all the banana mixture has been added, stir in the sultanas and walnuts or pecans.

4 Spoon the mixture into the loaf tin and bake for about 1 hour, or until a skewer pushed into the centre comes out clean.

5 Leave to cool in the tin for 30 minutes before turning out onto a wire rack and leaving to cool completely before peeling off the lining paper.

simply delicious

QUICK TIP... For a special treat, frost the banana bread with cream cheese icing. To make this, whisk together 125 g (4 oz) of cream cheese, 50 g (2 oz) of softened butter and 225 g (8 oz) of sieved icing sugar until smooth and creamy. Spread the frosting over the top and sides of the loaf with a palette knife.

SERVES 8–10

MIXING, FOLDING & KNEADING

Almost all recipes involve mixing ingredients together but, depending on the recipe, this is done in different ways. Bread dough and muffin batters have their own separate techniques to make sure they rise properly and are deliciously light and airy when baked.

EQUIPMENT NEEDED

MUFFIN AND CUPCAKE TRAYS

These trays can be made of metal or silicone, and contain 6 or 12 cups. Use a tray with large cups for baking muffins, medium cups for baking cupcakes and shallow cups for baking pastry tartlets.

MIXING BOWL

A large bowl used for mixing ingredients for making bread, muffin mixes, cookie doughs and cake batters.

CLING FILM

A thin, transparent film made of plastic, used for covering bowls and dishes or wrapping food to keep out the air.

MIXING

Mixing is half way between beating and folding. While beating involves a vigorous action and folding a very gentle one, mixing is combining ingredients by stirring them together with a metal or wooden spoon in a saucepan or bowl.

FOLDING

When you've whisked lots of air into egg whites so they are light and foamy, the last thing you want is to beat all the air out again. To fold them gently into another mixture, use a large metal spoon or spatula, moving it in the shape of a large figure-of-eight and stirring as lightly as possible. Continue to do this until everything is evenly mixed together.

Technique 1: FOLDING MUFFIN MIXTURES

For light-as-air muffins, it's important not to beat the ingredients together too briskly. Simply fold them together until the dry ingredients are just moistened by the wet ones.

1 Put the dry ingredients – flour, bicarbonate of soda, and sometimes spices and sugar – into a mixing bowl (sieving them together so they are evenly mixed if the recipe calls for it).

2 Whisk the wet ingredients – eggs, melted butter or oil, and milk or another liquid – together in a measuring jug.

3 Make a well in the middle of the dry ingredients and pour the wet ingredients into it.

4 Gently fold the dry and wet ingredients together using a spatula, large spoon or table fork until the dry ingredients are just moistened. Don't worry if there are lumps, these are fine.

5 Add the remaining ingredients, such as chopped nuts, dried fruits, grated carrots, fresh berries, mashed banana or chocolate chips, and give the batter one more gentle stir to mix these ingredients in. Again, don't worry about any lumps.

6 Put paper muffin cases in the cups of a muffin tray – this helps the muffins keep their shape as they bake – and spoon the batter into them, filling the cases almost to the top. You can also bake the batter in the unlined cups, but spray them with a non-stick spray before you spoon the mixture in.

7 Bake the muffins according to your recipe, until risen and golden brown. Cool them for 5 minutes in the tray before lifting them out and placing them on a wire rack. Serve the muffins warm or leave to cool completely.

Technique 2: KNEADING BREAD DOUGH

Few smells are as wonderful as homemade bread baking in the oven. All that's needed to make bread dough are four basic ingredients – flour, salt, liquid and a raising agent – and these haven't changed since the time of the Ancient Egyptians. Mix those ingredients together and follow a few simple rules, and your bread will rise to the occasion every time.

MAIN INGREDIENTS OF BREAD

FLOUR
Use flour labelled 'strong' or 'bread flour'. 'Strong' means that when the dough is kneaded, extra gluten is produced, giving the baked loaf a light, airy texture.

YEAST
This is used to make the dough rise. Fast-action or easy-blend yeast are the simplest to use and just need stirring into the flour.

LIQUID
This can be water or milk and, while it needs to be warm to encourage the dough to rise, it must not be hot or it will kill the yeast and your bread won't rise at all. The liquid needs to be 'blood' heat – 37°C/98.4°F – so, to check it is about the right temperature, dip a finger in and the liquid should feel very slightly warm.

SALT
A little salt helps the yeast work and gives your bread a better flavour.

1 Once you have made your bread dough (see recipe on page 60), it must be kneaded to work the gluten in the flour so the dough is smooth, elastic and will rise properly. Put the dough on a lightly floured board and stretch and pull it vigorously to develop the gluten. Use the heel of one hand to push it away from you and then fold it back towards you to make a ball, turning the dough as you work. You'll need to do this for about 10 minutes to get the dough to the right spongy texture.

2 When you've finished kneading the dough, shape it into a ball and place it in a mixing bowl that's been lightly brushed with oil to stop the dough sticking to it.

3 Cover the bowl tightly with cling film – brush this with oil too if you think the dough will reach the top of the bowl when it rises – and leave the dough in a warm place, such as a sunny room, until it has doubled in size, which will take about 1½–2 hours.

4 After the dough has risen, peel the cling film off the bowl and punch the dough back down with your fist. Knead it again on a lightly floured board for 1–2 minutes to disperse any air bubbles trapped in the dough.

5 Shape the dough into a rectangle and place it in a greased loaf tin. Alternatively, shape the dough into a round or cut it into small pieces and shape into rolls and place on a greased baking sheet.

6 Cover the shaped dough loosely with cling film – oil the cling film lightly to stop the dough sticking to it – and leave in a warm place for about 30–40 minutes until doubled in size again. The technical name for this second rising is called 'proving' and it ensures the baked loaf has a more even texture than if it were only risen once.

SEEDED BREAD ROLLS

These rolls can be eaten on their own with butter and jam, or you can use them to make a sandwich. They also go well with a steaming bowl of soup.

YOU WILL NEED

Board for kneading the dough

Cling film   Measuring jug

2 baking sheets, greased
Wire cooling rack

Mixing bowl   Spoon

Pastry brush

Knife

Measuring spoons

INGREDIENTS

- 175 g (6 oz) strong white bread flour, plus extra for kneading
- 175 g (6 oz) wholemeal bread flour
- 4 tsp caster sugar
- 1½ tsp fast-action dried yeast
- ½ tsp salt
- 150 ml (¼ pt) warm milk
- 40 g (1½ oz) butter, melted and cooled
- 1 egg, beaten
- sunflower or groundnut oil, for greasing the mixing bowl, cling film and baking sheets
- 1 egg yolk beaten with 2tbsp cold water, to glaze
- 1 tbsp sesame seeds
- 1tbsp poppy seeds

CHECK YOUR SKILLS

- p. 59 for kneading bread dough
- p. 42–43 for using the oven

p. 59 for kneading bread dough
p. 42–43 for using the oven

SERVES 10

1 Mix the white and wholemeal bread flours together in a mixing bowl and stir in the sugar, yeast and salt.

2 Make a well in the centre of the dry ingredients and pour in the milk, butter and egg. Stir with a spoon until evenly mixed and then press the dough together with your hands to make a ball.

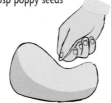

3 Transfer the dough to a board lightly dusted with flour and knead by hand for 10 minutes until the dough is smooth and elastic.

4 Place it in a mixing bowl that has been greased by brushing with oil, cover the bowl with cling film and leave the dough to rise in a warm place for 1½–2 hours or until it has doubled in size.

5 Punch the dough down with your fist and knead it again on a board for another 5 minutes. Cut it into 10 equal-sized pieces and roll each piece into a ball between the palms of your hands. Press the tops down lightly with your fingers to flatten them a little.

6 Divide the balls of dough between two greased baking sheets, spacing them well apart so they have room to rise. Cover with oiled cling film and leave to rise again for 30–40 minutes or until doubled in size.

7 Preheat the oven to 200°C/400°F/gas mark 6. Brush the rolls with the beaten egg yolk and sprinkle sesame seeds over half of them and poppy seeds over the other half.

8 Bake for about 20 minutes, or until golden brown, and the rolls sound hollow when tapped on the base. Slide onto a wire rack to cool.

TRY THIS!
Instead of shaping all of the dough into balls, roll some into thin sausages about 20 cm long and tie into knots.

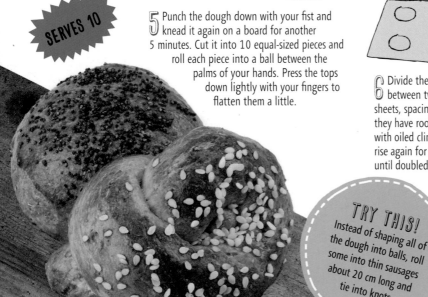

CHOCOLATE MOUSSE

Mmmm… this is the perfect dessert for chocoholics! This recipe uses a mix of milk and dark chocolate, but if you prefer a stronger flavour, use all dark chocolate.

INGREDIENTS

- 50 g (2 oz) butter
- 150 g (5 oz) milk chocolate chips
- 150 g (5 oz) dark chocolate chips
- 125 g (4 oz) white mini marshmallows
- 4 tbsp milk
- 300 ml (½ pt) double cream

YOU WILL NEED

Knife

Large heatproof bowl

Large metal spoon

Saucepan

Balloon whisk or handheld electric whisk

4 glasses or serving dishes

1 Cut up the butter into small pieces and put in a large heatproof bowl. Add the milk and dark chocolate chips, the mini marshmallows and the milk.

2 Fill a saucepan one-third with water, put it on the hob and bring the water to a simmer. Turn the heat under the pan down to low and sit the bowl on top of the pan, making sure the bottom of the bowl doesn't touch the water.

CHECK YOUR SKILLS

- p. 48 for melting chocolate
- p. 48 for using the hob
- p. 53 for whipping cream

3 In another bowl, whip the cream until it thickens and holds its shape.

4 Using a large metal spoon, fold the cream into the melted chocolate mixture until it is evenly mixed in and there are no white streaks of cream remaining.

TRY THIS! Decorate each mousse with a spoonful of whipped cream. Crumble a small chocolate flake and sprinkle that over the cream.

SERVES 4

5 Spoon the mixture into four glasses or serving dishes and chill in the fridge for 2–3 hours or until ready to serve.

QUICK TIP... If you can't find mini marshmallows, you can use large ones instead. Just snip them into small pieces with kitchen scissors first so they melt more easily.

CARROT AND PECAN MUFFINS

These muffins will get your day off to a great start! Have one for breakfast with a glass of fruit juice. You could also pack one for lunch or for a snack when you need an energy boost to keep you going until dinnertime.

YOU WILL NEED

12-cup muffin tray
12 paper muffin cases
Wire cooling rack
Skewer
Sieve
Mixing bowl
Measuring jug
Spatula, spoon or table fork

INGREDIENTS

- 275 g (10 oz) plain flour
- 1½ tsp bicarbonate of soda
- 1 tsp ground cinnamon
- 150 g (5 oz) caster sugar
- 150 ml (5 oz) sunflower or groundnut oil
- 3 large eggs
- 1 tsp vanilla extract
- 75 g (3 oz) chopped pecans
- 75 g (3 oz) sultanas
- 250 g (9 oz) carrots, grated
- 12 pecan halves

CHECK YOUR SKILLS

- p. 59 for folding
- p. 13 for grating

1 Preheat the oven to 180°C/350°F/gas 4. Line a 12-cup muffin tray with paper muffin cases.

2 Sieve the flour, bicarbonate of soda and cinnamon into a mixing bowl and stir in the sugar.

3 In a measuring jug, beat together the oil, eggs and vanilla. Fold into the dry ingredients until just mixed in, using a spatula, spoon or fork.

4 Stir in the pecans, sultanas and grated carrot.

5 Spoon the mixture into the muffin cases and bake for 20–25 minutes or until risen and golden. A skewer pushed into the centre of a muffin should come out clean.

QUICK TIP... Although the muffins are delicious eaten plain, you could also spread the tops of them with cream cheese icing (see Banana Bread recipe on page 57).

6 Cool in the tray for 15 minutes before carefully lifting the muffins out. Serve them warm or transfer to a wire rack to cool completely.

MAKES 12

GLOSSARY OF EQUIPMENT

BOARDS For cutting and chopping. Keep separate boards for fruit and vegetables, fish, meat and bread. Wash and dry thoroughly after use.

CAKE AND TART PANS These come in many different shapes and sizes, can be deep or shallow and made of metal or silicone. Place silicone pans on a metal baking sheet before spooning in the batter.

CASSEROLE A large, deep ovenproof pan with straight sides and a tight-fitting lid, used for slow-cooked dishes such as stews.

CLING FILM A thin transparent plastic film that 'clings' to surfaces and itself. Used to cover bowls and dishes and to wrap food.

COLANDER A large bowl-shaped utensil with holes, used for draining foods such as pasta, vegetables and rice.

COOLING RACK This allows air to move around baked goods as they cool to stop condensation forming and making them soggy. Choose a rack with a narrow grid so small items don't break or fall through.

FISH SLICE A utensil with a long handle and a flat, blunt blade with holes. Used for turning food, particularly fish, and to lift and drain items from a pan when cooked.

FOIL A thin metal sheet of aluminium used for wrapping food in an airtight parcel to keep it fresh. Also used for lining grill pans and covering a dish in the oven to prevent the top browning.

GARLIC PRESS A handy utensil for crushing garlic. Cloves are pushed through the press by squeezing two handles together, the skin remaining in the press while the clove is squeezed out as a purée.

KITCHEN PAPER Food-safe absorbent paper used for lining plates to drain excess fat from fried foods and general kitchen jobs such as wiping utensils or mopping up spills.

LADLE A large spoon with a cup-shaped bowl and long handle used for serving sauces and soups.

MEASURING JUG A glass or plastic jug with marks up the side for measuring liquid and dry ingredients.

MEASURING SPOONS A set of different sized spoons for measuring liquid and dry ingredients in quantities of 2.5ml (½tsp), 5ml (1tsp), 10ml (1dsp) and 15ml (1tbsp). Dry ingredients should be level with the top of the spoon.

MIXING BOWL Used for beating egg whites, whisking cream and tossing salads, as well as mixing ingredients for cakes, cookies and doughs.

OVENPROOF COOKWARE Any dish or tray made of ceramic, cast iron, silicone or metal that is used for oven cooking. Examples include muffin trays, casseroles and roasting tins. Always wear oven gloves when taking a dish out of the oven.

PALETTE KNIFE A knife with a long, flexible blade and rounded end that bends easily. The blade has no sharp edges and is used to spread frostings and cake fillings and for smoothing toppings such as mashed potato.

PASTRY BRUSH Available with silicone or natural bristles, these food-safe brushes are used for tasks such as glazing pastry with beaten egg or milk and greasing tins. Wash well after use and dry before storing.

ROLLING PIN A long, heavy cylinder made of wood, marble, stainless steel or plastic, used for flattening or rolling out dough.

SCALES For measuring quantities of ingredients needed for a recipe.

SIEVE Similar to a colander but with a finer mesh, used for sieving dry ingredients to remove lumps, sauces and soups to make them smooth, and soft fruits to remove seeds.

SKEWERS Made of wood or stainless steel. Small similar-sized pieces of raw food are threaded onto the skewers to make kebabs. Wooden ones need soaking for 30 minutes to prevent them burning.

SPATULA A thin flat tool made of wood, silicone or metal with a broad, blunt blade. Used for mixing, spreading, turning food in a frying pan and stir-frying.

TONGS Large, two-handled pincers for turning burgers, sausages and other meats on a grill or barbecue or in a frying pan, lifting long pasta and corn cobs from a pan of boiling water or for serving salads.

WOODEN SPOON A good alternative to a metal spoon when cooking as it doesn't get hot, nor does it scratch a pan with a non-stick coating. Also used for beating cake batters or stirring ingredients together.

INDEX

Apple Tarts 17
Apricot Coulis with Yogurt and
    Toasted Oats 50

baking 42, 43, 46
baking parchment 43, 54
baking sheet 42
    lining 43
baking tin 42
Banana Bread 57
beating 52, 54, 56, 57
beef, browning 31, 33
Beef Tacos 33
biscuits, crushing 19
blenders 24, 25
boiling 36, 39
bread crumbs 19, 20
bread dough 60
    kneading 59
browning 31, 33
butter and sugar, beating 52

cake mixture, beating 52, 54
cake tin 42
    lining 43, 54
Carrot and Pecan Muffins 62
carrots, peeling and cubing 7
cheese, grating 13
Cheese Omelette 56
Cheese Straws 15
Cheesy Stuffed Potatoes 28
chicken, roasting in foil 43
Chicken Satay 45
chillies 26
chocolate, melting 48
Chocolate Chip Cookies 46
Chocolate Mousse 61
Chocolate Sauce 48
Chocolate Sponge Cake 54
chopping boards 4, 6
citrus juice presses and extractors
    18, 19
cling film 58, 59
coulis 49, 50
cream, whipping 52, 53
crudités 10
crushing 18, 19, 22
cucumber batons 12

eggs
    poaching 36, 37, 38
    separating 53
    whisking egg whites 52, 53, 55
Eggs Benedict 38
equipment 5

fish fingers 20
folding 58, 61, 62
food hygiene 4, 31
food processors 18
French Toast 34
Fresh Lemonade 23
fruit
    coulis 49, 50
    juicing 16, 18, 19, 23
    puréeing 25
    smoothies 29
    zesting 13, 23
Fruit Coulis 49
frying 30, 33, 34–5
    stir-frying 30, 32
frying pan 30

graters 12
grating 12–13, 14, 16, 35
grill rack 42
grill tray, setting up 42
grilling 42, 44–5
Guacamole 26

halloumi 47
Hash Browns 35
Homemade Fish Fingers 20
Hummus 27

juicing 16, 18, 19, 23

kebabs 14, 45
Key Lime Pie 16
kneading 59, 60
knives
    safety 4, 6
    types of 6
    using 6–11

Macaroni Cheese with Cherry

Tomatoes 51
mashers 24
mashing 24, 25, 26, 28
measuring jug 48
Meatballs in Tomato Sauce 21
milk pan 48
Minestrone Soup 9
Mini Pitta Pizzas 44
mixing 58
mixing bowl 58
muffin and bun trays 58
muffin mixture, folding 58, 62

New York Cheesecake 22

onions
    sautéing 31
    slicing 7
oven gloves 4
oven safety 4

pasta 8
boiling 36, 39
peelers 12
peeling 12, 17
Perfect Pasta with a Creamy
    Mushroom Sauce 39
poaching 36, 37, 38
Pork Kebabs with Mint and
    Cucumber Raita 14
preparation 5
puréeing 24–7, 29, 49, 50

rice, steaming 41
Rich Tomato Sauce for Pasta 8
Roasted Mediterranean Vegetables
    47
roasting 42, 43, 47
roasting tin 42

safety in the kitchen 4, 6, 30, 36
sandwich pan 42
sauces 48–51
    lumpy 49, 51
sausages, frying 30
sauté pan 30, 31, 36
sautéing 30, 31
Seeded Bread Rolls 60

soups, blending 24
Steamed Asian Dumplings 40
steaming 36, 37, 40, 41
Stir-Fried Chicken with Cashews 32
stir-frying 30, 32
Strawberry and Banana Smoothie
    29
Strawberry Pavlova 55
Super Fruit Salad 11

tasting food 5
Tex-Mex food 33
tidy working habits 5
tomato wedges, cutting 6

Vegetable Fried Rice 41
Vegetable Platter 10
vegetables
    grating 35
    mashing 25
    roasting 47
    steaming 37

whipping 52, 53, 55, 61
whisk 48, 52
whisking 52, 53, 55
White Sauce 49
wire sieve 48
wok 30
wooden spoon 52

yeast 59

zesting 13, 23